architecture design data

T0373372

Phillip G. Bernstein

architecture

Practice
Competency
in the Era
of Computation

tec

ture

design

data

Birkhäuser
Basel

To my always supportive family, and architects worldwide who work every day to make the world a more livable and valuable place.

Contents

Preface

*Making is a matter of feeling, not thinking: just do it. Does it break?
Try again... and again... and again. Or even better, let the computer try
them all (optimize).*
Mario Carpo in *The Second Digital Turn: Design Beyond Intelligence*[1]

In 1990 I was a young architect working for Cesar Pelli when we purchased
our first raft of personal Compaq computers, each equipped with an early
version of AutoCAD along with an equally expensive HP plotter. It was an
exciting time, because the transition from hand drafting to computer-aided
design (CAD) felt important, a move into the modern age. Of course, architects were decades late to the party of the first digital turn, waiting for the
curves of descending cost and ascending graphic capabilities to cross. And
now we had a fleet of exotic machines, each of which cost as much as a decent car, sitting behind our drafting tables, and we wasted little time putting
them to work.

   During a project review with Cesar we plastered an entire wall of the
studio with a series of plotted plan explorations, neatly organized by series (1,
2, 3, etc.) and then sub-options (A, B, C), using our new toys to demonstrate
how thoroughly we had explored this particular problem. Cesar, decidedly
nonplussed about the work, declared that we were confusing drafting with
thinking, and declared, as he examined our 50-odd options, that we were "using the computer for the systematic generation of useless alternatives."
Ouch.

   Technology certainly does not replace thinking, but it may change
the frame in which it happens, for better or worse. In the intervening years
since our comeuppance from Cesar, a lot of digital technology has made its
way onto the studio floors of the world's architects, but few of the fundamen-
tals of the architect's work or role in the overall systems of project delivery
have changed, with the possible exception of certain formal opportunities to

---

1   Mario Carpo, *The Second Digital Turn: Design Beyond Intelligence*, "Writing Architecture," (Cambridge, MA: The MIT
     Press, 2017), p. 163.

generate and manage complex geometry. Early digital tools like 3D modeling and scripting have yielded some compositionally exuberant results, but done little else to empower architects to function in the increasingly complex environment of building, where speed to market, sustainability requirements, automation on the job site and digital building control systems — to name just a few of the things making our work so much more complex — raise the expectations of owners, increase our liability and consume time and effort, which are increasingly less available from the tighter, more competitive fees that resulted from the global economic crisis of 2008.[2]

The Second Digital Turn

We may be, however, at a tipping point in the equation that balances the architect's agency and methodology of design with the potential of what Mario Carpo has called *The Second Digital Turn*, or the era of intensive computation. The space between the first turn (computer-based geometric modeling) and the second (cloud-based, big-data-enabled machine learning and artificial intelligence) was bridged by another technology, building information modeling (BIM). As the price/capabilities curves of personal computers brought very powerful desktop machines with graphics processors to the architect's and engineer's studio, building design could move from tools that simply described geometry to those that brought an understanding of a building to bear on the problems of design and construction. Where once a computer represented a wall or a window as a three-dimensional collection of lines projected (even at full scale) in space, that same wall or window in BIM understands its construction assembly and relationship to floors, walls and other building systems. Despite BIM's immediate utility as a technical drawing generator (it produces perfectly coordinated drawings as an artifact of a single data representation of the building) its real importance, potentially, is as an epistemological structure upon which lots of other smart computation — including machine learning and simulation — can be built.

The early days of BIM — from 2002, when Autodesk made the Revit acquisition and declared a strategic shift away from AutoCAD, through 2009, when large numbers of American architects began to adopt BIM[3] — included much discussion about how the technology might be weaponized in the war of control between architects and contractors. Each side declared that the power of BIM information gave them primacy in the struggle for superiority in the design-to-build process. As adoption became widespread, however, and enthusiasm tempered by the downturn of 2008, both architects and contractors began to work through the questions of what sort of information

2   Email conversation with the author and AIA Chief Economist Kermit Baker, January 2018.
3   BIM adoption in the US is measured in various ways, varying mainly by the definition of BIM and what software is connected to its alleged use. A more sophisticated model is based on tool usage, as described in Wooyoung Jung and Ghang Lee, "The Status of Bim Adoption on Six Continents," *International Scholarly and Scientific Research & Innovation* 9, no. 5 (2015).

was useful during design and construction, and how it might best be exchanged cooperatively to the benefit of the project. Builder-owners and managers, in a moment of clarity, declared through a manifesto that improvement was a function of owner-driven innovation in information and risk sharing enabled by new technologies like BIM.[4]

New delivery structures like integrated project delivery (IPD) emerged, but little else changed on the broader playing field. Customers and technologists alike realized that design models (like those created by BIM) and construction models (those necessary to build) were different animals, and that a more complex and nuanced set of solutions was going to be necessary to reach the integrated digital promised land.

With the informational infrastructure of BIM creating a reference framework for design, and cloud computing providing the computational and storage firepower necessary to wrangle the enormous datasets that are needed to represent buildings, we are coming to a time where technology and thinking are perhaps not so separate anymore, and a need to re-examine the methodologies of design is apparent. How does the complex of information that results from the digitization of design create both opportunities and threats for architects? This question is largely unanswered in an age of high-resolution building models disgorged by the architect's normative practice with BIM today. Simulation and analysis, soon to be bolstered by machine learning, create a design environment where a range of outcomes, from cost conformance, constructibility and code compliance through to, eventually, occupant behavior can be predicted *a priori* and those predictions can be used to hone the design. This structure of looped analysis and insight will make it possible to optimize any design in ways only the most experienced architects could have achieved today — and none will be able to achieve tomorrow unless assisted by technology.

That same ability to generate and study alternatives and predict performative outcomes gives architects a far more potent tool to enhance our role in delivery structures than could have ever been anticipated by the 'BIM data control' arguments of fifteen years ago. Understanding and prediction are precedent to making business commitments and structuring the architect's agency, and compensation based on predicted outcomes — rather than commoditized promises of limited fees — changes the very value proposition of practice itself.

With our new machines years ago, we took advantage of the capabilities of an emergent CAD platform to design a curving laboratory building on

4   Construction Users Roundtable (CURT), "Collaboration, Integrated Information, and the Project Lifecycle in Building Design, Construction and Operation," in *CURT Whitepapers* (Construction Users Roundtable, 2004). In this whitepaper, a building owners' association declared that four changes in industry practice were necessary: owner leadership, integrated project structure, open information sharing and use of virtual building models.

a very tight site, something that would likely have been impossibly complex and time-consuming if drawn by hand. Of course, little did we know that every single sheet of the resulting hundreds of working drawings would take as long as 12 hours to output, with one of us supervising the oft errant plotter. Technology gives, and it takes away.

In *The Second Digital Turn* Carpo imagines a time when traditional scientific knowledge is replaced with gigantic datasets of experience, indexed in such a way that science and engineering return to the more heuristic approaches of craftsmanship — trying things just to see if they work, but letting the computer generate the alternatives. The maker simply 'feels' that a solution is right, and if not, the computer just generates another attempt. For as long as architecture has an ineffable dimension, architects will continue to rely on feelings and instincts, but unlike the past, those instincts will be well-supported by computational assurances, especially for the aspects of building where, technically or otherwise, risk is high. With instincts backed by support along both axes, architects will be empowered. This book outlines some theories and strategies for architects to maintain and expand their expertise as designers of the built environment.

0.1

0.1 Boyer Center for Molecular Medicine, Yale University by Pelli Clarke Pelli Architects

1

introduction

1.1

A Systemic Transformation

The Second
Machine Age

In their seminal exploration of the importance of technology, *The Second Machine Age*,[1] MIT's Brynjolfsson and McAfee argue that the advent of ICT (information and communication technology) is as significant a development in human progress as the steam engine. The construction of modern buildings would not be possible without the successors to those engines, but similar reliance on ICT has only now begun in earnest, in the first two decades of the twenty-first century. This is not to suggest that certain forms of digital technology — primarily drafting and rudimentary communication tools, like CAD and email — were not important earlier, but it would be difficult to argue that they have had transformative effects on the role of architects or the process of designing and making buildings. If anything, effects have been formal and compositional, leading to more complex, expressionistic shapes and a more intricate interweaving of systems. In this spirit, software for building is largely created for, and used by, architects and engineers toward these relatively straightforward ends. Yet other fundamental human endeavors are dramatically changed in the second digital turn. Modern financial systems are entirely reliant on high-speed, global ICT infrastructure. Agriculture and manufacturing are both heavily automated, having moved far beyond the machinery of the first industrial revolution. Medicine depends on high-resolution imaging, electronic medical records, big data analysis and increasingly on robotic methods in the surgery suite. With these changes in technology came similar transformations in process, professional methodology and production as well as roles, obligations and values.

The second digital turn: cloud-enabled big data and machine learning

This book will argue that a similar systemic transformation is underway in the building industry, with particular implications for architects. The canonical obligations of the architect — to coordinate a project to manifest 'design intent' in order to enable a builder to create the actual, physical asset — are evolving in an era where information, insight and predictions generated during design move into construction no longer essentially via drawings but other, more profound media. The structures of design, production

---

1   Erik Brynjolfsson and Andrew McAfee, *The Second Machine Age: Work, Progress, and Prosperity in a Time of Brilliant Technologies* (New York: W. W. Norton & Company, 2014).

and delivery themselves will transform as a result, and this book proposes to create a framework within which those changes can be understood and explicitly managed by a profession which must become better equipped to direct its future.

The cloud: delivering hosted computation and storage over the internet

With the advent of increasing connectivity and the computational power and storage capacities of the cloud, new technological capabilities greet today's architect in waves. High-resolution modeling and simulation, 3D printing, robotics, drones and the internet of things are some of the innovations with potential to empower but also disrupt processes of design and construction. In their above-mentioned book, Brynjolfsson and McAfee suggest that combinations of these technologies — rather than single tools — are the sources of real innovation and change, catalyzed by the new-found capabilities of this second digital turn.

Building information modeling as a general purpose technology

Architecture has been in the thrall of the digital for decades, inheriting and repurposing technologies created for other ends. Drafting tools built for engineers became the CAD platforms that replaced manual drawing. Form-generating tools created for the gaming industry were adapted to generate and manage complex geometry. The first major built-for-purpose technology to invade architecture was arguably building information modeling (BIM), which presaged the shift from orthogonal two-dimensional representation of buildings through drawings to three-dimensional digital simulations of a design, a change that occurred three decades ago in manufacturing and product design. Like many disruptive innovations, BIM was first put to best use, ironically, in the service of enhancing established methods, in this case creating more accurate technical drawings. Widely adopted today, BIM has become what Brynjolfsson and McAfee call a 'general purpose technology,' in that it is used to support the building design, construction and building operation. However, in combination with the cloud, another general purpose technology, BIM enables profound changes in how design happens, and what design may mean. Under the influence of these developments, projects will rely less on the intuition and judgment of designers (who are held personally responsible for the implications of the use of that intuition) and more upon predictive strategies of how a building will actually look, operate and feel when complete. As a consequence, substantial changes in the roles of the architect, the methodologies of practice and the relationship of design to the delivery systems of construction — value propositions, in current parlance — will evolve. Eventually, architecture will, in a sense, 'catch up' with other disciplines, professions and institutions that are fully engaged in the second digital turn.

Agency, methodology, value

These changes will be both evolutionary and revolutionary, and in order to best explain them the book proposes two organizational strategies. On the first level, it will explore technology through the lenses of agency (what is the role of the architect and what does the architect control?);

methodology (what are the processes of design most concerned by transformation?); and finally value (what does the architect deliver to the system of building and how is it valued, socially and financially?). On a second level, each of these topics will be examined in the course of time: historically, establishing the arc of current practice, and then speculatively, defining transformations and their implications.

Design, technology and professional practice are largely taught separately in today's schools of architecture. Design studio is a pedagogical platform in and of itself, while both technology and practice are taught as support courses — or not at all. Professional practice classes are often a litany of war stories and management strategies, disconnected from any other aspect of the design curriculum. Many aspects of professional education outside the studio are driven by the external demands of practice and licensure, creating a strange divide between the core value proposition of architecture (creating a design) and the agency of the architect (actualizing that design for a client). What is more, architectural education today largely treats digital tools as mechanisms for making artifacts, without much context as regards their implications in the broad world of practice, where recent graduates are the most technologically skilled and, at the same time, the least experienced members, while their elders, who make the important decisions in an architecture practice, are the opposite. The most technologically skilled members of practice are often those with the least understanding of the implications of those tools. This text argues that all architects — both the next generation and their mentors — must understand and correlate our role in future practice as design agents empowered by technology within the economic and technical systems of delivery, and undertakes to create a framework to build that understanding.

2

agency

2.1

The Digital Transformation of Design

How does technology change architectural process by refactoring the means of representation and design reasoning, and the relationships between the architect and others in the building process?

> *In the Renaissance, as now, new information technologies, instead of building technologies, were the agents of change. New information technologies brought about some new devices of design that in their turn revolutionized the process of building and changed architectural forms.*
> Mario Carpo in "Building with Geometry, Drawing with Numbers"[1]

At its core, architectural design is speculation. The architect, charged by a client to translate aspiration to form, navigates two speculative leaps in the service of the project: projecting the experience and operation of the building when it is in use by creating the design, and converting the design into a built artifact. While the client is most interested in the former, it is the route to the latter that constitutes the core value of the architect's services in that the architect is absolutely necessary for that conversion. Design reasoning is the means to both of these ends, supported by instruments of representation and analysis.

Representing and reasoning about design

As explored in this text, 'representation' means the ways by which a design is depicted, explored, illuminated and communicated. Over thousands of years of designing and building, the drawing has been the prime means of such representation. Drawing gives architects a portable, inexpensive means to explain a complex, enormous thing like a building using the abstraction of graphics. In the development of civilizations, architects developed over time specific languages of building expression, graphical coding systems of sorts, by which the basic dimensional, formal and technical aspects of a building design could be explained. Constructs like the (floor) plan, building eleva-

---

1   Mario Carpo, *The Second Digital Turn: Design Beyond Intelligence.*

tion, cross-section and specific details evolved as a language of representation. As buildings and the systems by which they were created become more complex, so did the means of representation necessary to create them. In this way, representation and creation are intricately linked. This tradition goes back centuries, with a particularly beautiful example in Figure 2.1.1, a drawing by Robert Symthson that describes both the expression and fabrication strategy for a complex, double-curving window.

<u>2.1.1</u>

2.1.1 Robert Smythson, "A Rounde Window in a Rounde Wall" of 1599

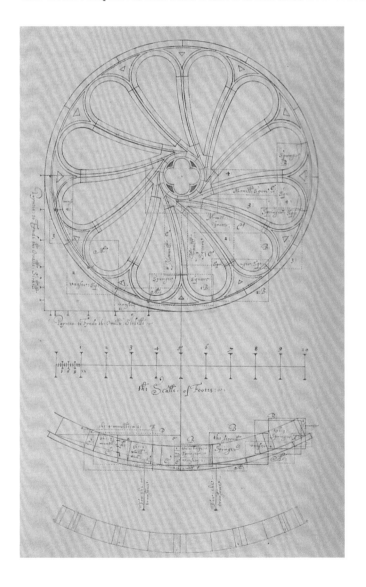

'Analysis,' or the process by which the implications of a design are explored, has relied almost exclusively on the experience and intuition of designers, augmented by mathematics, prior to the digital age. Medieval builders, who considered Euclid a mason and surveyor,[2] deployed tools of geometry to project the dimensional characteristics of early buildings, a crude early 'analytical model' that both asserted the structure's physical characteristics and allowed for the necessary abstractions to put the design on paper. The results were generated by geometric formulas. As the discipline of engineering emerged, analytical models were instantiated with formulas and standards, using the parameters of a project as inputs and using the outputs as preliminary validations of the characteristics of the design. Formulas could project rationalized conclusions about things like structural spans, deflection of columns, air temperature or required water volumes. But these analytical procedures were largely limited to the realm of design problems characterized by Horst Rittel and Melvin Webber[3] in 1973 as 'tame' — solvable through linear, systematic analysis grasped and deployed by trained professionals. Peter Rowe, in his subsequent application of this thinking to architectural design, suggested that the real purpose of design was to wrestle with what Rittel and Weber called 'wicked problems,' and these are the challenges that rely on the designer's experience, judgment and intuition:

The 'wicked' and the 'tame'

> Architectural design problems can also be referred to as being "wicked problems" in that they have no definitive formulation, no explicit "stopping rule," always more than one plausible explanation, a problem formulation that corresponds to a solution and visa versa, and that their solutions cannot be strictly correct or false. Tackling a problem of this type requires some initial insight, the exercise of some provisional set of rules, inference, or plausible strategy, in other words, the use of heuristic reasoning.[4]

2.1.2

Before geometry-based computational simulations replaced human calculation, analysis was performed by solving formulae, as shown in Figure 2.1.2.

So in the pre-digital age it was pretty easy to identify and characterize both the means of representation (drawings) and techniques of analysis (formulas and protocols), both of which were generated and managed by completely manual processes. This setting was enhanced with the availability of printing (and paper) in the Renaissance. More than five hundred years later,

2   Anthony Gerbino et al., *Compass and Rule: Architecture as Mathematical Practice in England, 1500–1750* (London, Oxford, New Haven, CT: Yale University Press; in association with Museum of the History of Science; in association with the Yale Center for British Art, 2009), pp. 17–18.
3   Horst W. J. Rittel and Melvin M. Webber, "Dilemmas in a General Theory of Planning," *Policy Sciences* 4, no. 2 (1973).
4   Peter G. Rowe, "A Priori Knowledge and Heuristic Reasoning in Architectural Design," *Journal of Architectural Education* 36, no. 1 (1982).

2.1.2 Analytical formulae

Problem to be solved	Example formula	Note
Compute moment in a simple beam, uniformly loaded	M_{max} (at center) $\ldots\ldots = \dfrac{wl2}{8}$	5
Flow resistance of air through a small opening in an exterior wall	$S_h(V) = \dfrac{p}{0.845 \cdot A^2} \cdot V$ where S_h is the flow resistance [Pa·m³/s] p is the density of the air [kg/m³] A is the area of the hole [kg/m²]	6
Required capacity of rainwater downpipes and gutters	$Qh = (a \times i) \times (\beta \times F)$ a = the reduction factor for the rain intensity for flat roofs a = 0.60 flat roof with ballast of gravel a = 0.75 for the other flat roofs As flat roofs discharge the water at a slower pace, for all other cases (therefore all pitched roofs) applies a = 1, i = rain intensity and is 1.8 (litre/minute)/m² β = reduction factor for the roof width is determined by the pitch roof F = surface of the roof	7

new digital platforms based on principles of computation are transforming the means of representation and analysis once again, and with them the role of the architect in the systems of building delivery writ large. And along the way, the once clear boundary condition between 'wicked' versus 'tame' problems will be redefined as well.

Computation emerges in the building industry

Like most things in the building industry[8] this change is slow but steady. The advent of the computer itself made barely a ripple in design and construction due to the enormous cost and complexity of available machines through the mid-1980s. As computation became democratized when personal com-

5 American Forest and Paper Associatation, "Beam Design Formulas with Shear and Moment Diagrams," http://www.awc.org/pdf/codes-standards/publications/design-aids/AWC-DA6-BeamFormulas-0710.pdf.
6 Axel Berge, Analysis of Methods to Calculate Air Infiltration for Use in Energy Calculations, Thesis, Chalmers University, 2011, http://publications.lib.chalmers.se/records/fulltext/147421.pdf.
7 Nedzink Company, "Determining the required capacity of rainwater downpipes and roof gutters," http://www.nedzink.com/en/info-and-advice/roof-drainage-system/112/determining-the-required-capacity-of-rainwater-downpipes-and-roof-gutters.
8 In this text, the term "building industry" refers to the network of organizations, participants and supply chain connections (including clients, designers, builders, fabricators and suppliers) necessary to deliver built artifacts into the economy.

puters became widely available, the first hints of process change emerged. Hand-typed specifications and project correspondence gave way to word-processed text; accounting and eventually cost estimating transferred from ledger sheets to spreadsheets. By the mid-1980s, the first graphics and CAD programs ran on computers that were affordable and available to architects and engineers; these platforms largely replaced their heavier, more expensive mainframe and mini-computer predecessors by the early 1990s, and the digital age in design was under way in earnest.

In the intervening decades there has been a veritable explosion in digital instruments available to the architect and her collaborators. In order to build the argument outlined above with more precision, we need to expand the broad categories affecting design processes beyond just representation and analysis, namely to include two additional process typologies: realization (the transfer of information between the digital and the physical worlds) and collaboration (the means by which the various players in the design/construction delivery continuum access, organize and transact information). In these four categories of representation, analysis, realization and collaboration (represented in Figure 2.1.3), digital tools act in concert to change the reasoning, role and responsibilities of the architect.

The evolution of representational technologies from the 1970s to the turn of the century has been explored extensively elsewhere and will not be the subject of this discussion.[9] It will suffice here to say that these histories correlate the evolution of computational mathematics and associated representational software with corresponding changes in the form-making potential of the architect, in both shape and manufacturing technique. Computers empowered both architects and builders to understand, manipulate and manage very complex, especially curving forms during design, fabrication and construction. The resulting co-dependence between data generator (the architect) and data consumer (the fabricator) presages changes in the relationship between the two that digitally empowered delivery models anticipate today.

Representation, analysis, realisation, collaboration

2.1.3

Digitized documentation

In that first iteration of digital technology in design, computers were used primarily in the service of a more sophisticated generation of form and the documentation of design through geometry. To the extent that it became easier to draw (and, allegedly, build) curving walls, facades and roofs, also conventional — dare I say mainstream — architects transitioned from hand drawings to computer-aided design (CAD). Drawings were generated by software like Autodesk's AutoCAD or Bentley's Microstation, text and numbers

9   For a complete if personalized examination of this question, see Greg Lynn's series of exhibitions in the Canadian Centre for Architecture's project "Archaeology of the Digital" and the associated publications.

How are ideas defined and memorialized?

(Models, metadata, drawings)

REPRESENTATION

How are ideas simulated and evaluated?

Simulation, analysis, scripting, optimization

ANALYSIS

How are ideas translated from digital to physical form?

Construction planning, procuring, assembling

REALIZATION

3D printing
Robotics
CNC/CAM
Laser scanning
Commissioning

COLLABORATION

How are ideas captured, managed and shared?

Reference data   Project record   External knowledge

by software like Microsoft Word and Excel. Even though the transfer from the analog to the digital was in some sense complete, all three techniques — writing, drawing and calculation — ultimately manifested in Renaissance results: printed on pieces of paper before real use, particularly in a client meeting or on the construction site. Maybe this was not such a big change after all.

Interestingly, there is an argument to be made that spreadsheet software was as important during this time as was CAD. While organizing and systematizing the various numbers that support an architectural design (space requirements, code calculations, cost estimates, project management budgets), Excel gave architects important capabilities in the two other tool buckets of analysis and realization. In the same way that the business world relies on spreadsheet-based financial models to test the implications of various decisions, so could architects and their collaborators build various analytical models of those 'tame' aspects of the design subject to mathematical evaluation. Energy models, cost estimates, space allocation tracking and other structured numerical problems yielded easily to the increased ubiquity of the PC-based spreadsheet, to their benefit.

2.1.4

Technology Category	In the pre-digital age	In the early era of CAD
Representation	Hand drawing, typed text	CAD drafting, word processing, spreadsheets (tables)
Analysis and Simulation	Formulas, experience, intuition	Early computational analysis software, spreadsheets (calcs)
Realization	Physical translation of construction approach from drawings	Transfer of numerical control information from CAD geometry
Collaboration	Catalogues, telephone, tables of standards, postal and overnight services, faxing	Email, file servers, online databases, FTP

See also 2.1.6, p. 28

That same utility, the systematic organization and structure of the spreadsheet, also provided an important conduit of design data from the designer to the fabricator. Complex curving shapes described in the computer were based on underlying mathematical models, like splines and NURBS, that were otherwise impossible to document in the traditional form of two-dimensional projections with measurements on pieces of paper. No matter how many dimension lines the architect overlaid on the drawing of the blobby form she was creating, the fabricator was still largely at sea trying to understand how to build it. Shop drawings, the fabricator's attempt to describe in detail back to the designer how something was to be assembled, introduced more time and transactional friction to the process. To the rescue came spreadsheet software, where complete spatial coordinates (X, Y and Z planes) could be extracted, compiled and transmitted to a fabricator from the original design model. In this sense, spreadsheets were the first realization tools available to the building industry. This method used data instead of graphics to bridge intent to execution. Other more robust tools and strategies were to follow.

Shop drawings: detailed drawings of the assembly approach used for fabrication

Divisions of labor

While this numeric means of jumping the gap between design speculation and built artifact gave some early adventuresome architects and builders and fabricators a chance to cooperate directly,[10] the industry writ large remained hewed to traditional models of collaboration dictated by similarly hidebound roles and responsibilities. Designers still were responsible for creating something called 'design intent' — a speculative description of a project as it might be once built — and contractors for 'the means and meth-

Architecture, engineering and construction (AEC) industry

---

10 Probably the most well-known example of such an architect is Frank Gehry, whose firm pioneered both new formal ideas and the technologies and business models necessary to create them.

ods of construction' — translating that design intent into all the processes, procedures, supplies, contracts and assemblies that result in a finished building. Under this model, which largely persists today, responsibilities and exchanges of information are carefully parsed along the lines of perceived risk of a lawsuit, with said risk management often taking a higher priority than the requirements of the project itself.

Digital means of collaboration, as another category in the design process, lagged behind its representational and analytical counterparts, particularly in the age of early CAD where there were few means to transmit the large files necessary to describe a complex building. Until the advent of an internet where larger files could be exchanged, 'sneaker nets' of floppy disks, often moving via overnight courier, connected project teams who otherwise communicated by phone and fax machine. Up-/download times over telephone lines made the physical transmission of digital media more reliable and often faster.

On balance, the computerization of design in these early stages felt important and disruptive to the architects, as if we were finally entering the modern age of computers. But those who implemented it relied strongly on long-established analog methods: drawing things, direct face-to-face communication, moving physical artifacts like disks and computer plots. Strategies for delivering projects remained largely the same.

From digital drawings to simulative models

In this context, various types of design-enabling technologies are evolving rapidly, and with them important implications for the architect.

Representation has largely transfigured in modern construction economies from drafting-centric tools of CAD to building information modeling (BIM), software that creates three-dimensional, behaviorally simulative digital *doppelgänger* of the design from which the drawings are extracted like reports from a database. A correspondingly dramatic increase in available information — both precise geometry coordinated in three-dimensional space, and associated metadata[11] — can now be created by the architect.

Metadata: data about the data

Analytical tools, empowered by cloud computing, stretch across a spectrum of project characteristics from testing structural integrity to evaluating sustainable Triple Bottom Line impacts,[12] further accelerated by the resulting collection of big data that can be leveraged for future evaluation. Those tools will soon shift from fixed algorithms (where evaluation is predetermined and instantiated into the software code itself) to machine learning, AI-based validation based on neural networks able to adapt evaluation crite-

Triple Bottom Line evaluation

11 Metadata, or 'data about the data,' refers here to the additional information associated in BIM with a given represented element. For example, the shape, depth and configuration of a door comprise its geometric data; the door's fire rating, construction type, cost of installation and associated hardware would be considered metadata.
12 "Triple Bottom Line" economics is a theory that suggests that sustainably designed buildings have three benefits which must be considered, measured and balanced for success: financial, social and environmental.

ria. The pipeline between the digital and physical has widened in both directions: for example, model-based design information more easily transits to computer-controlled fabrication equipment (when the business conditions are right), while high-res three-dimensional scanning allows users to easily integrate documentation of existing physical conditions into digital design. Documentation, design resolution and, eventually, fabrication and construction are accelerated as a result.

Finally, high-capacity, ubiquitous connectivity and online storage are a platform for a new generation of physically separated but informationally integrated teams, where designers or builders can be pretty much anywhere. Technology provides so many toys, and potentially tools, and with them, many opportunities.

These technologies portend a potential seismic shift in both process and role for architects. First, and perhaps most obviously, more enabled tools make it more likely that architects can keep up — or even set the pace for — the design of today's increasingly complex buildings that demand more exacting and complete information to actuate. If they act as the professionals at the center of the design process, architects empowered with new technologies have the opportunity to remain the integrator and coordinator of an ever-increasing retinue of specialty consultants and building technics requirements. The resulting infrastructure of information that comprises the design deliverable is of enormous potential use to builders and fabricators, who are turning toward computationally driven industrialized construction techniques based on huge collections of data which could be delivered by the architect and her consultants.

Intent versus
execution Today's traditional delivery systems separate the responsibilities of the architect (intent) from those of the builder (execution), either in concept or in practice or both. The polarity of this relationship will reverse, bringing closer interdependencies between architect and builder, entailing new contractual, risk and compensation models that more accurately reflect the value of the combined effort. The emergence of integrated project delivery models (see Chapter 3.3: "Designing Design: Optimizing, Solving, Selecting"), catalyzed by the possibilities of BIM, is but one example of this change. Delivery models themselves have evolved in parallel with technologies — at least in the US — as described in Figure 2.1.5.

2.1.5

Project delivery models, the organizational structures that establish the business relationships between owners, architects and contractors, have been elaborated decade by decade, starting in the 1970s when almost every project was "good old-fashioned Design Bid Build," where builders were selected based on lowest cost. But the economic context of a given decade are the precedent to the evolution of the next model in the following ten years. In the 1980s, very high interest rates drove construction to be as fast as possible, creating the idea of fast-tracked construction management.

2.1.5 The evolution of project delivery models, 1970–2020

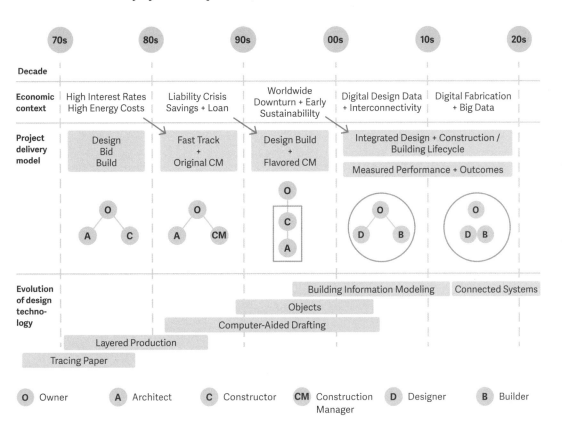

	70s	**80s**	**90s**	**00s**	**10s**	**20s**
Decade						
Economic context	High Interest Rates High Energy Costs	Liability Crisis Savings + Loan	Worldwide Downturn + Early Sustainabililty	Digital Design Data + Interconnectivity	Digital Fabrication + Big Data	
Project delivery model	Design Bid Build	Fast Track + Original CM	Design Build + Flavored CM	Integrated Design + Construction / Building Lifecycle Measured Performance + Outcomes		

Evolution of design technology:
- Tracing Paper
- Layered Production
- Computer-Aided Drafting
- Objects
- Building Information Modeling
- Connected Systems

O Owner A Architect C Constructor CM Construction Manager D Designer B Builder

The liability crisis of the 1980s led to consolidated lines of contract responsibility (where clients could file one single lawsuit) and thus to Design Bid Build. Deep collaboration, made possible by BIM in 2000, opened up the possibility of integrated project design. In the future, analysis and simulation will further drive outcome-based delivery models, bringing the owner, architect and contractor even closer together in integrated models yet to be seen.

Predicting outcomes of design and construction

Construction itself is notoriously challenging and risky, and the industry is rife with studies about degrees of low productivity, inefficiency and unpredictability. Labor productivity in construction has remained flat for decades,[13] and industry efficiency itself is generally considered to be around 65% per dollar spent on the job site in the US. Business deals for designers and builders are almost always based on promises of lowest first cost, and

---

13 See Paul Teicholz, "Labor-Productivity Declines in the Construction Industry: Causes and Remedies (Another Look),"
in *AECbytes,* March 14, 2013, http://www.AECbytes.com/viewpoint/2013/issue_67.html, and McKinsey Global Institute,
"Solving the Productivity Puzzle: The Role of Demand and the Promise of Digitization" (2018).

Technology Category	In the era of BIM modeling	In the era of machine learning
Representation	Parametric models of geometry and metadata	Artificial intelligence-informed design through interlinked digital models
Analysis and Simulation	Digital analytical models tied to scripts that test and choose results	Big data-based neural networks that predict complex outcomes
Realization	Model-based simulation of construction yielding build-ready data	Information originating from the design process drives self-learning automated machinery on the project site.
Collaboration	Web-based, social-media-enabled real-time connection and data exchange.	Real-time interaction enhanced by virtual and augmented reality supplemented with predictive collaboration through AI.

See also 2.1.4, p. 24

such commoditized environments not unexpectedly create razor-thin profit margins that further dis-incentivize innovation. Many of these problems result from the speculative gap between design and construction, and many design and build teams struggle to translate their design objectives into processes that can meet owner objectives, including budget and schedule. Predicting these things in concert is devilishly challenging, and thus results in the risky and litigious environment that dominates today.

But what if the informational and analytic infrastructures evolving from today's technologies — which put simulation and prediction on the basis of computation, big data evaluation, even machine learning — shifted the essential organizational structures of the building process? Instead of assembling teams with delivery systems connected by promises of lowest costs, those models could be based on predictive outcomes: essentially promises to deliver a project with specific performative characteristics. Those characteristics, agreed upon in advance by the team and the client, would be correlated directly, as incentives, with paying fees connected to accomplishing them, and their predicted outcomes would be deeply understood from the representational, analytic and realization capabilities provided by emergent technologies. Meeting technical challenges in terms of budgets, schedule and energy usage are first-step changes in the transformation, but as computers enhance our powers of analysis, simulation and optimization, the objectives of building can be more complex and interesting, stretching to building performance and human experience. Thus the architect, empowered with the necessary tools to make the view across the speculative gaps much more clear, moves closer to the act of construction, embraces

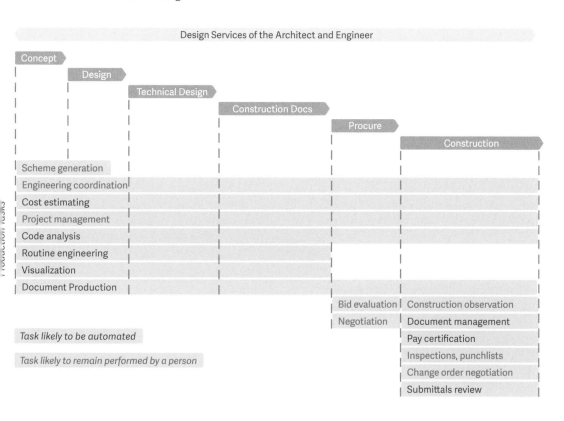

Design Services of the Architect and Engineer

	Concept	Design	Technical Design	Construction Docs	Procure	Construction
Scheme generation						
Engineering coordination						
Cost estimating						
Project management						
Code analysis						
Routine engineering						
Visualization						
Document Production						
					Bid evaluation	Construction observation
					Negotiation	Document management
						Pay certification
						Inspections, punchlists
						Change order negotiation
						Submittals review

Task likely to be automated

Task likely to remain performed by a person

2.1.6 and manages the risks of results, and changes her value proposition to the entire enterprise of building.

In his interpretation of Rittel and Webber's 'tame' versus 'wicked' problems, Peter Rowe did not address the 'tame' components of the design process per se. In the aggregate of the design process, 'wicked' comprises a large number of 'tame' problems solved by procedural and analytic means. The more prosaic components of working out a building design — laying out a toilet room, organizing a door schedule — are hardly wicked. Where such knowledge was once the exclusive province of experienced designers, it can now be recorded and accessed digitally in the form of parametric models and scripted generational procedures. Some of these procedures are hard-wired into representation engines; any decent BIM software can easily generate a simple door schedule. Scripting languages today encode the designer's knowledge of manipulation, usually of geometry, and those scripts are often paired with analysis programs that evaluate the output. An energy use simulator might be paired, for example, with a modeler that is using a script to test different massing forms, simultaneously generating the building

2.1.8 'Wicked' vs. 'tame' problems

'Tame' design challenges	'Wicked' design challenges
Computing areas	Choosing a design strategy for the overall organization of the building
Determining toilet capacities	Making tradeoffs between ambiguous priorities
Coordination of structure and mechanical systems for clashes	Managing client expectations
Checking shop drawings for geometric conformance	Composing the aesthetic expression of an element, space or building composition
Counting and coordinating electrical fixtures	Translating design intent to the contractor

shape and telling the designer the resulting energy use implications. There is a direct business need to face this question of 'wicked' vs. 'tame' problems with clarity: about 40% of an architect's fee[14] in a typical project is assigned to portions of the work that are mostly 'tame production' (such as working drawings) and that work is likely to be automated in the future. Figure 2.1.7 speculates which of the architect's responsibilities, across the spectrum of typical services, are likely to be automated.

2.1.7

Taming wicked problems

Clearly the boundary between 'wicked' and 'tame' problems is starting to blur, and the tamer the problem, the more likely it is to be assigned to a competent computer. While this suggests a reduced need for architects working in the realm of the tame, my earlier argument — that we could have a greater role in outcomes paired with a deeper connection to fabrication and building — may offset the loss, much like when industrialized machinery began to replace farm workers in the twentieth century, many of those farm workers found jobs in the factories that made the equipment. The strategy must be one of replacing the evaporating value proposition of production work like creating construction drawings with a different one, such as computationally supported, outcome-based delivery, including a deep connection from design to making.

14 The largest portion of an architect's services (and fee) are related to the technical delineation of the project and related production tasks necessary to complete a detailed specification that articulates the design intent for the builder. In the United States, such work can comprise as much as 40% of that effort (say, half of the design development phase which comprises 20% of the fee, and most of the construction documents phase which comprises 35% of the fee). These are the first parts of architectural work likely to be automated, with a concomitant reduction in necessary work.

Finally, Rowe's conclusion that solving 'wicked problems' requires the use of heuristic reasoning is today cautionary rather than reassuring. In the era of computation, surely only humans can accomplish those tasks that require heuristics, techniques that build on experience and trial and error — finding 'answers that work.' And yet, perhaps the most important emergent technology to affect all knowledge work does not fit neatly into our categories of technologies affecting design, but rather cuts across them all: machine learning. The victory of IBM's Watson over the reigning Jeopardy champion in 2011[15] presaged the widespread commercial availability of computers capable of learning, reasoning inferentially and drawing complex conclusions. IBM sells Watson as a platform now, and machine learning technologies that use neural networking techniques to study large lakes of data to build an understanding of a given knowledge set already have applications in the building industry. A recent research project, for example, uses machine learning to examine thousands of construction records to predict risk factors for projects.[16] Turning the attention of such technology on the burgeoning data sets that are today's computer-enabled design/construction projects will have obvious implications for the wicked aspects of both design and construction. Machines will learn to design, and fundamentally change the design process.

2.1.8

I have argued elsewhere that architects should embrace, rather than be threatened by, the growing role of computation in design,[17] and five years after making that case I still endorse it, if for slightly different reasons related to the emergent need to proactively address the emergence of machine learning. Buildings will continue to increase in complexity, as technical, economic, social, even aesthetic phenomena and the design process must progress in concert, with the resulting challenges. Being an architect will thus entail facing and solving far more 'wicked problems' in the future, likely challenging the capabilities of even the most accomplished artificial intelligence-based design system. If we can deploy emergent technologies in the service of, rather than as a replacement for, our abilities to attack wicked problems we may well have a better chance of solving them. Our responsibilities to the building process will evolve accordingly.

15 "IBM's Watson Supercomputer Destroys Humans in Jeopardy," https://www.youtube.com/watch?v=WFR3IOm_xhE.
16 In this project, a group of contractors pooled project information across hundreds of jobs to provide a big data source for analysis. See Autodesk BIM 360 Glue, for example https://knowledge.autodesk.com/support/bim-360-glue/learn-explore/caas/video/youtube/watch-v-nuWlpqevflk.html.
17 Phillip G. Bernstein, "Digital Workflows Book Launch." In 100, edited by Columbia GSAPP Lecture (New York, NY: Columbia University GSAPP, 2013).

2.2

Defining Design Intent: Depiction, Precision and Generation

How does technology change reposition design information (and design responsibility) relative to creation of a completed artifact and redefine the concept of design intent?

2.2.1 Cover of Alberti's *L'Architettura*

2.2.1

Architects often hark back to the simpler times of the so-called 'Master Builder,' when a single individual controlled all aspects of building-making. In that putative era — think Brunelleschi and the Florentine Duomo during the Renaissance[18] — the transmission of information from designer (the architect) to executor (the builder) was relatively simple because roles were conflated, buildings relatively straightforward (by modern standards) and schedules often stretched to decades. It was Alberti, working at the same time as Brunelleschi, who suggested that ideas were artifacts of their own, separate from buildings, and that there was a specific role in creating those ideas, to wit, the professional architect. The architect was responsible, as described and translated by Mario Carpo, for giving the builder "sound advice and clear drawings" which said builder was to follow without deviation. This advice allegedly ended at the completion of the design. As Carpo describes Alberti:

> *Designers first need drawings and models to explore, nurture, and develop the idea of the building... (those) models should also be used to consult experts and seek their advice; as revisions, corrections and new versions accumulate, the design changed over time; the whole project must be examined and re-examined... The final and definitive version is attained only when each part has been so thoroughly examined that any further addition, subtraction or change could only be for the worse.*[19]

The act of design itself forms a project, according to Alberti, "conceived in the mind, made up of lines and angles, and perfected in the learned mind and

18 Ross King, *Brunelleschi's Dome: How a Renaissance Genius Reinvented Architecture* (New York: Walker & Co., 2000).
19 Mario Carpo, *The Alphabet and the Algorithm*. "Writing Architecture" (Cambridge, MA: The MIT Press, 2011).

2.2.2 Execution and efficacy gaps

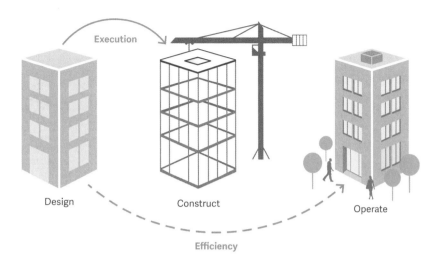

imagination."[20] Further, once those repeated revisions and refinements were completed and the drawings and models handed over to the builder, "no more changes may occur"[21] and the builder is to proceed exactly as instructed. Of course, once the roles of designer and builder are distinct, it is incumbent on the former to communicate ideas with clarity to the latter (and everyone else) so as to reach this Albertian state of design-to-construction fidelity.

Design and the architect's intent

The demand that the design communicate intent clearly remains despite the obvious fact that the environment in which we build today differs enormously from Alberti's time. Buildings are more complex in form, performance requirements, use and interaction of materials, relationship of systems, regulatory constrains (like sustainability), even aesthetic expression. Where in the past all responsibilities were conflated in the Master Builder, today's projects have specific roles, relationships, responsibilities and standards measured by professional commitments and certification, legal standards and evolving methodologies of design and construction. Rivers of information created by the architect course throughout the project, intended to communicate the evolving design and, ultimately, the intention for the final result. This vision of the project, and the various mechanisms meant to allow others to understand it, is what we call 'the architect's design intent.'

Design intent

The definition of 'design intent' is not, surprisingly, explicit in practice standards as provided in contracts, but architects Atkins and Simpson pro-

20 Leon Battista Alberti, *On the Art of Building in Ten Books*. Transl. Joseph Rykwert, Neil Leach and Robert Tavernor (Cambridge, MA: MIT Press, 1988).
21 King, *Brunelleschi's Dome*.

vide a cogent explanation of the distinction between the obligations of the designer and the builder:

> *it's evident that the architect's drawings alone cannot be used [for building by the contractor] because they are conceptual in nature and inherently inadequate for that purpose. If design drawings were sufficiently complete and adequate for construction, there would be no need for the general contractor. The architect would be providing the plan for putting the work in place... In developing a 'complete set of instructions for building the building' the architect would already have determined the means and methods for placing the work.*[22]

This is a modern explanation of a very old idea. Since the Enlightenment, design intent has been articulated to the constituents of the building process — including various collaborators and consultants, decision-makers, regulators, purchasers, administrators, suppliers and builders — using physical (models), textual (writing) and graphical (drawings) tools that were largely stable until the advent of digital technologies in the late twentieth century.

Instruments of service

Irrespective of format, these various outputs are termed 'instruments of service' in modern parlance to denote that they are not products in and of themselves but rather vectors by which design intent is transmitted, as a result of the architect's professional judgment, to any consumer of said information. That judgment is exercised in the creation of the design itself. In one sense, the architect's design intent is comprised of her 'vision' of the project, that coordinated, three-dimensional conception of the building as a physical object that exists *in toto* only in her mind's eye, at least before construction begins. It cannot possibly be complete, as the final product is comprised of thousands of pounds of materials, many more interrelationships and often unexpected or unanticipated conditions.

In another sense, that vision is an assertion about the way the building will appear and operate as a place for human occupancy, function and aspiration. Along the way, design intent must transform from a representation to a built artifact that can then be occupied. Thus the architect has two overall strategic objectives in generating 'design intent': to jump from the

Execution to
efficiency gap

2.2.2

'learned imagination' into construction (the 'execution gap') and into a finished object in a state of use (the 'efficacy gap'). Digital technology restructures both the strategy and for outcomes of each of these jumps.

22 James B. Atkins and Grant A. Simpson, *Managing Project Risk: Best Practices for Architects and Related Professionals* (Hoboken, NJ: Wiley, 2008), p. 138.

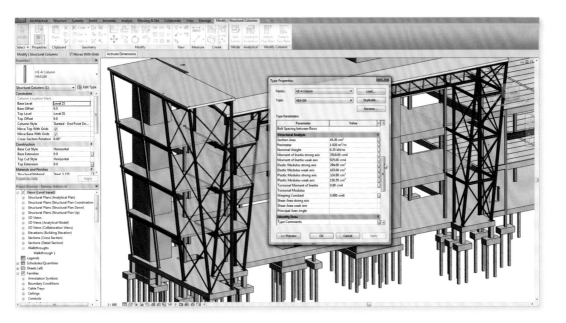

Design depiction and analysis

The advent of building information modeling represents a quantum leap in depictive power. At a basic level, BIM-based design was the first step in more directly connecting the architect's vision of the building to its realization without the intermediate step of orthographic projections like plans, sections or elevations. Describing the design as a model allowed such projections, still very necessary to the design process, to be extracted from a three-dimensional digital manifestation of the building. Further, the BIM representation conflates graphic and notational information about the design, as the digital representations of discrete elements of the building (such as a door, wall or window) include not just their spatial locations but also metadata — characteristics like weight, size, energy performance — and, by implication, the relationships between these data with other building elements. Processes that were computationally challenging in a world where all design intent was graphic, like quantity take-offs or area calculations, become by-products of the design process itself.

Information about building elements is stored in a building information model as data that can be displayed in various ways, including as a three-dimensional projection and characteristics of a specific element, as 2.2.3 shown in the BIM screen shot in Figure 2.2.3.

More importantly, a building designed with BIM gives the designer a powerful new platform to enhance and accelerate her judgment and improve the design. Those models are, in part, behaviorally provocative simulations

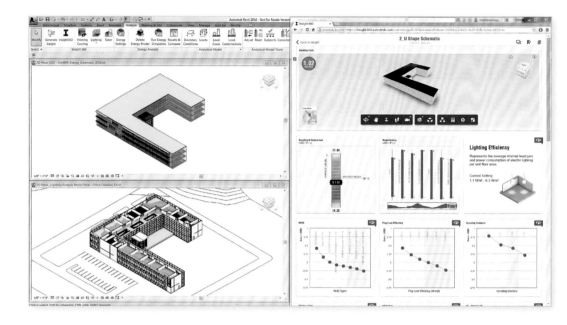

of the emerging building itself, and thus tools that can be interrogated, iter-
ated rapidly to enhance Alberti's recommendation that the building be "perfected in the learned intellect and imagination."[23]

Combined with the extended power of cloud computation and the
arrival of an arsenal of simulation tools that analyze and evaluate the implications of model behavior, the tools of design intent are extended from mere
depiction to prediction – from the depiction of a vision to the prediction of a
future reality. For centuries of building, architects and engineers used experience, judgment, intuition and some procedural knowledge (like formulas)
to project the performance of building. The arrival of both analytical software and machine learning based evaluation of real world data extends the
designer's capabilities for prediction enormously; prediction now becomes
an explicit component of the expression of the design, instantiated into the
instruments of design intent themselves.

Depiction to prediction

2.2.4

Design generation

But architects have never relied, in the digital turn, exclusively on algorithms
provided by software providers. Since the early days of programs like Auto-
CAD, designers could roughly automate certain procedural design approaches by scripting drafting commands with the software that made the
drawings. This strategy has been dramatically extended in the twenty-first

---

23 Carpo, *The Alphabet and the Algorithm.*

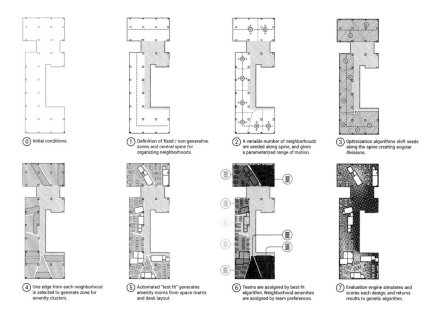

⓪ Initial conditions.

① Definition of fixed / non-generative zones and central spine for organizing neighborhoods.

② A variable number of neighborhoods are seeded along spine, and given a parameterized range of motion.

③ Optimization algorithms shift seeds along the spine creating angular divisions.

④ One edge from each neighborhood is selected to generate zone for amenity clusters.

⑤ Automated "test fit" generates amenity rooms from space matrix and desk layout.

⑥ Teams are assigned by best-fit algorithm. Neighborhood amenities are assigned by team preferences.

⑦ Evaluation engine simulates and scores each design, and returns results to genetic algorithm.

century through a discipline called 'computational' or 'generative' design, where complex scripts manipulate digital geometry and give architects mastery over forms previously too mathematically and graphically challenging to accomplish by human hands and brains alone.

In the digital turn, algorithms allow designers to combine the representational potency of BIM and the evaluative opportunities of predictive analytical software for a third component of design intent: generation If simple scripting can create a wide range of geometric options for a given design problem, more complex generative strategies reframe the proposition of design intent itself. The range of possible options is greatly expanded, the opportunity to explore far more alternatives engaged and the likelihood of new solutions enhanced. The evolution of a range of planning solutions, generated via algorithm, is shown in Figure 2.2.5.

2.2.5

And since designing a building comprises solving an array of problems from the sublime to the ridiculous — or, as Rittel might suggest, from the 'wicked' to the 'tame' — the application of these combined techniques will likely begin with tamer problems while releasing the designer's energy to focus on the more wicked.

Let us speculate about the following example of a BIM-based design process where the assignment is to design a small community library for a public client. The architect is trying to find an appropriate concept that meets certain constraints: the project brief calls for a modest reading room plus shelving for a small collection within a relatively tight budget and stringent energy performance characteristics. The architect creates a simple BIM with adjustable parameters for the building's dimensions (including height), site orientation and access strategy. She decides that the primary variables are building dimensions, orientation toward the sun and the ratio of glass openings to solid wall, and she wants to understand the code, energy and cost implication of several alternatives, so she deploys the following tools:

— **Building information modeling** as the primary representational platform
— **Analytical software** for cost estimating, energy analysis and building code evaluation
— **A scripting platform** like McNeel's Grasshopper or Autodesk's Dynamo
— **A reference library** of the architect's past projects, residing on the firm's servers

She first scans her library of past projects with a machine learning routine that suggests key performance characteristics of a successful design, and she tweaks these conclusions to suit the constraints of the current assignment. Then a simple generative script that varies her key parameters creates a wide range of alternatives, many of which fall outside the performance boundaries returned by the analytical software, helping pare the possibilities. The toolkit above has expanded the range of possible solutions (using a 'tame problem' strategy) and likely not yielded a 'correct' answer (because that is a 'wicked problem') but has certainly expanded her understanding of the range of solution ideas.

Two of the more intractable aspects of the design challenge — systematically generating alternatives that might be interesting, and fully evaluating each for cost, code and energy — have been automated. The objectives of the design process itself were established from both the client's brief and past history of other projects; in the past, only the former would have been an explicit requirement. The process of establishing design intent — and the instruments of service themselves — have expanded to explicitly include depiction, prediction and generation.

Evolving methods of determining intent

Depiction, prediction and generation

Given the inexorable march of technology, it is likely that this rather mild example represents just the beginning of the tripartite (BIM, analytics, scripts) evolution of new strategies to generate design. Each category — depiction, prediction and generation — will continue to increase in capacity, capability and implication. While it is unlikely that drawing itself will ever disappear from architecture — it is far too efficient and effective — the design ideas that result, ultimately, in those depictions will be more accurate and of higher fidelity. The ability to represent a building in far greater levels of detail will increase with computation and storage capacity, and depiction will no longer be constrained by the need for abstraction (unless this is necessary for a given moment in the design process). As computational modeling becomes more robust, models themselves will include or connect to other digital representations of building components, thereby providing insight into assembly, installation, maintenance and operational data.

Predictive tools, which are today largely software that applies vast computational resources to complex analytical algorithms, will be enhanced by the insights gained by collecting, measuring and evaluating actual results of design decisions. Today IBM advertises how its machine learning platform Watson can predict the performance of a basketball player or the productivity of a vineyard *a priori*, presaging the widespread availability of such capabilities. This will be an enormously important tool in the built environment where there are literally millions of functioning examples — operating buildings — in existence and available for indexing, reference and insight. Common design errors that are the result of the failure to predict how something is built, used or behaves will be reduced or eliminated.

Generative design approaches that do the 'heavy lifting' of alternative creation will combine with predictive tools to expand the range of possible solutions, as schemes can be more systematically explored by algorithmic generation. As a precondition, framing a design problem so it can be properly evaluated computationally will become as important as the creative process of finding the solution. Designer heuristics will transition to the 'wicked problems' of framing design parameters and the strategies for exploring solutions rather than generating them. Defining the design problem by setting its parameters, as inputs into the generative tools, will rise in importance relative to the actual process of solving the design problem.

Bridging intent to execution

Demand for digital design information to drive increasingly automated construction inexorably draws the architect and builder together. Depiction will include not just information about a given architectural element's geometry and physical state, but the implications of how it should be made and what it will do once it is in place. Providing this information will certainly not replace what Atkins and Simpson declare as the fundamental responsibility of the architect to monitor design intent, but rather inform the creation of design information while smoothing its route to the job site.

The architect 'Master Builder' of yore based decisions almost exclusively on experience, judgment and intuition. Pre-digital architects, with shorter deadlines and much more complicated projects, worked much the same way, outsourcing the 'prediction' of technical performance to consultants and generating solutions to 'wicked problems' heuristically. Second-era digital tools, evolving in the way suggested here, will shift the architect's role, responsibility, and the underlying presumptions of the efficacy of design intent itself.

Modern architects have had, at best, an ambivalent attitude to jumping the execution gap, working in uneasy relationships to construction. Architects see involvement in construction as a risky, unpredictable proposition with little upside, and as a consequence are parsimonious with the information they generate during design. At the same time, builders often cite "unusable architect's documents"[24] as a primary reason for their difficulties, and rare is the builder who truly understands the difference between the architect's obligations to create 'design intent' documents versus 'construction planning' documents,[25] although they are, in fact, completely different things. But construction will eventually yield to the improvements made possible by digital, robotic or automated production and the inputs to those processes begin with the architect. To maintain strategies where that information is either firewalled from the builder, or worse, replicated in low fidelity, hardly advances the causes of efficiency or effectiveness. Higher-fidelity depiction and more accurate prediction make the digital assets of design intent production very valuable to builders, reducing risk and thereby beginning to close that execution gap, which (as I have argued elsewhere[26]) is a fundamental barrier to effective construction.

Execution to operation

Standard of care

Bridging the efficacy gap proves, in the long run, to be the most important objective in the restructuring of design intent. Modern society relies on the expertise of professionals to guide it through complex, specialized undertakings like design. The legal standard by which the performance of the architect is measured, the standard of care (see Chapter 2.3, "The Evolution of Responsible Control and Professional Care") essentially defines competency as the sound judgment in a situation according to which an otherwise capable architect would have operated. One might argue that sound judgment is the fundamental value of a good architect, and what clients ultimately are looking for when they ask for professional help.

Clients have many motivations for creating buildings: artistic expression, embodiment of values and social role, even brand. These are the more 'wicked' aspects of a designer's obligations. But every client, save the pure patron of the arts, also wants a platform for living, working or other activity and sees a building as an enabler of those aspirations. Anticipating how a building operates as a living, breathing and occupied organism comprised of spaces, light, materials, energy and other systems is a fundamental value de-

24 Harvey M. Bernstein, "Managing Uncertainty and Expectations in Building Design and Construction," in Harvey M. Bernstein (ed.), *McGraw Hill Smart Market Reports* (New York: McGraw Hill Construction Analytics, 2014).
25 Atkins and Simpson, *Managing Project Risk*, p. 138.
26 Phillip G. Bernstein, "Thinking Versus Making: Remediating Design Practice in the Age of Digital Representation," in Branko Kolarevic and Kevin R. Klinger (ed.), *Manufacturing Material Effects: Rethinking Design and Making in Architecture* (New York: Routledge, 2008).

livered by architects. The evolution of tools that more precisely depict the intent of the design and make its performative outcomes more understandable and, even more importantly, more likely to be achieved, can not only improve the reputation of architects but enhance our value in the creation of the built environment.

The inherent dangers of such an approach, where the fundamental value of an architect shifts to her ability to predict the future of her building, are twofold. As a profession we must take care not to allow prosaic, procedural and analytic issues to overwhelm the expressive and ineffable qualities of architecture, lest we find ourselves living in a world of machine-generated blandness. There is surely enough of such "systematic" building lining the commercial strips of today's cities, where the architect's only value seems to have been to sign and seal drawings that resulted in a building permit.

The secret here is to assure that the inherent potential of new depictive, predictive and generative tools is to create new, unseen and important opportunities for innovation, progress and expression. High-resolution rendering, big data analytics and algorithms in general may yield, ultimately, higher-quality results by virtue of the opportunities of precision and simulation. If those things do not give the architect first more productive cycles, and second, more insight to use in defining and elegantly solving the 'wicked' challenges of architecture, then we will have, as a profession, squandered an opportunity not likely to be offered again. But more importantly, as the tools that yield the results of design become more sophisticated, insightful and automated, it will be equally important to apportion our efforts and reaffirm the 'wicked' nature of design itself. Buildings, like all things made by humans, sometimes demand simple and uninteresting solutions that instruments of the 'tame' can surely solve, particularly if those buildings do not require human habitation (think data centers or warehouses). But otherwise our profession must deploy these new-found capabilities in the service of ever-improving architecture.

2.3

The Evolution of Responsible Control and Professional Care

In what way does the professional role of the architect evolve in the digital age and how does this affect normative measures of competency and related legal standards?

> *All technical submissions, which are (a) required by public authorities for building permits or regulatory approvals, or (b) or intended for construction purposes, including all addenda and other changes to such submissions, shall be sealed and signed by the architect. The signature and seal may be electronic. By signing and sealing a technical submission the architect represents that the architect was in* responsible control *(emphasis added) over the content of such technical submissions during their preparation and has applied the required professional standard of care.*
> National Council of Architectural Registration Boards (NCARB),
> Legislative Guidelines[27]

The National Council of Architectural Registration Boards (NCARB), a consortium comprised of 54 state/protectorate architectural licensing boards in the US, provides its members with model legal guidelines to create local regulations that govern the practice of architecture, from which the quote above has been excerpted. These guidelines represent the consensus thinking, a 'national sense' as it were, of how architectural practice should be defined, regulated and administered. The quote describes a central concept, a *raison d'être*, at the heart of the state's interest in creating professional architects: "responsible control," wherein a specific person granted the status of "architect" must both control and take responsibility for the technical delineation of an architectural project. A competent architect maintains this "responsible control" over a project during its design (and in some jurisdictions, construction) in order to assure the public's heath, welfare and safety. Unpacking the real implications of this concept, which is present in many coun-

27 *National Council of Architectural Registration Boards, Legislative Guidelines and Model Law — Model Regulations 2016–2017* (Washington, DC: NCARB, 2016), p. 17.

tries in different forms, in the second digital turn is central to understanding and defining the current and future role of architects in the systems of delivery that create buildings.

Allocating responsibility

The existence of architectural licensing regulations presumes that the state has a vested interest in creating safe and appropriate buildings for the use of the public and that professionals are necessary to assure that this is accomplished. Not unlike doctors or lawyers (who presumably protect the public's health and legal rights, respectively), professional architects serve the public in two important ways. First, they are expected to have the experience, education and certification that demonstrate a degree of competence sufficient to protect the public's health, safety and welfare.[28] Second, and equally important, an architect delivering her services toward this end must do so as an individual who can be held personally responsible for that competence. Professional services are thus distinct from, say, creating and selling a product, in which a customer purchases a thing like a car or television from a corporate entity that produces it. In the rare cases where that thing might cause harm, the corporation (and not its managers or employees) is held responsible. While the contractor for the project makes a product — the building — the architect provides services to assist the client in getting that building to happen.

Protecting the public is the main reason for licensure

Thus architects, in reality, render their judgment and cannot distance or disabuse themselves of personal responsibility for the results. Society has decided, through regulatory structures and law, that such professionals, in exchange for the tremendous freedom and responsibility offered by their trade, must be 'on the hook' for the resulting consequences. Professionals are expected to be personally competent.

Defining competence

But the state regulations do not stipulate what competent practice looks like, nor are they in any way specific about the performance requirements for professionals much beyond the description of responsible control above. A professional can only be 'measured' in comparison with other practitioners — under a challenging concept called "the Standard of Care," defined as follows:

Standard of Care

> *The Architect shall perform its services consistent with the professional skill and care ordinarily provided by architects practicing in the same or similar locality under the same or similar circumstances. The Architect shall perform its services as expeditiously as is consistent with such professional skill and care and the orderly progress of the Project.*[29]

28 The standard or duty of care has similar definitions in the United States and the United Kingdom.
29 Dale L. Munhall, "Standard of Care: Confronting the Errors-and-Omissions Taboo up Front," *AIA Best Practices* (February 2011), p. 1.

In other words, the competence of the architect's work is measured by somehow comparing it to what others in similar situations would have done, as likely measured in court under threat of a negligence lawsuit. Many such lawsuits stem from issues far beyond questions of the public's health, safety and welfare but rather result from disappointments in the execution and delivery of a building on the part of contractors and clients, usually associated with broken budgets, schedules or technical failures. (Questions of negligence and professional liability are further explored in Chapter 3.6, "Opportunities, Risks and Rewards.") An 'ugly design,' unless it somehow compromises building codes or otherwise threatens the public, is not a breach of the standard of care.

The state enforces its interest in protecting the public's health, safety and welfare by (1) establishing and regulating the profession of architecture (and limiting who can call themselves an architect), (2) stipulating that performing the services that architects provide is the 'practice' of architecture, and (3) requiring that documents that have been certified by a professional architect ('signed and sealed,' in popular parlance) are required before the state will authorize construction of a building by issuing a building permit. It is a common misperception that the main thing that distinguishes an unlicensed 'architectural designer' from a 'real registered architect' is that seal. Practicing architecture is providing the broad spectrum of services described in the traditional phases like schematic design, design development, and so on — and doing so without a license is a violation of the statutes. Signing the final working drawings precedent to applying for a building permit is just the final step.

Delivering expertise   Of course, many 'products' are created as the architect delivers her services: drawings, reports, models, data files and renderings, to name a few. These artifacts, however, are better known as "instruments of service"[30] precisely because they are not ends in themselves, but rather the conduits by which professional judgment is delivered. Despite efforts by clients to own these artifacts, national law based on an international treaty (The Berne Convention for the Protection of Literary and Artistic Works of 1886), in this case the US Architectural Works Copyright Protection Act of 1990, stipulates that the architect remains the owner of her instruments of service, and provides a license to users of those items — engineers, contractors or clients — to provide others with access.

---

30 "Instruments of Service" are defined in US contracts as follows: "representations, in any medium of expression now known or later developed, of the tangible and intangible creative work performed by the Architect and the Architect's consultants under their respective professional services agreements." American Institute of Architects, *A201 2007 General Conditions of the Contract for Construction* (Washington, DC: American Institute of Architects, 2007), p. 9.

The architect's preparation of any document requiring her signature and seal must include putative supervision and control over the preparation of that document in order to directly connect the responsibility of the architect for competence to the underlying mechanisms of delivering her judgment. NCARB provides the following definition of "responsible control" in their guidelines:

> *That amount of* control over and *detailed professional knowledge of the content* (emphasis added) *of technical submissions during their preparation as is ordinarily exercised by a registered architect applying the required professional standard of care, including but not limited to an architect's integration of information from manufacturers, suppliers, installers, the architect's consultants, owners, contractors, or other sources the architect reasonably trusts that is incidental to and intended to be incorporated into the architect's technical submissions if the architect has coordinated and reviewed such information. Other review, or review and correction, of technical submissions after they have been prepared by others does not constitute the exercise of responsible control because the reviewer has neither control over nor detailed professional knowledge of the content of such submissions throughout their preparation.*[31]

A chain of opportunity, certification and responsibility can be see in these related concepts: the state fulfills a social need for appropriate buildings (to protect health, welfare and safety) by creating a class of professionals (via licensure) who are responsible for their design (professional liability). Ideas about that design are articulated by various means (the instruments of service), and competence is measured accordingly (the standard of care). The architect's fundamental responsibility in these arrangements is predicated today on the concept explained earlier (see Chapter 2.2, "Defining Design Intent"), having defined that intent during the design phases of the work, enforced it during construction in collaboration with the builders and cemented it to the requirement of personal responsibility by obliging the architect to directly supervise design work (responsible control).

In the pre-digital era, each of these concepts was stable and clear. Professional training was founded on the basic division of labor (design versus execution) between the architect and the builder. Instruments of service were hand-drawn, sketched or sometimes typed, and relatively limited in scope and detail. In fact, the concept of responsible control was understood

---

31 National Council of Architectural Registrations Boards, "Model Regulations," *Legislative Guidelines 2014–2015* (Washington, DC, 2015), p. 16.

to require that if as the architect you did not draw something yourself, you directly supervised the individual who did so.[32] 'Plan stamping' — the practice of hiring an outside architect to swoop in at the end of the design process and stamp a set of drawings — directly violates the concept of responsible control and is considered a breach of professional conduct.

Devolving responsibilities

Two critical changes began to transform these relationships in the US in the 1980s: the professional liability crisis,[33] and the advent of first-generation computer-aided drafting. In the first case, an explosion of lawsuits against designers and builders was precipitated by a change in social norms related to access to the court system. Deregulation of professional ethical standards related to advertising and pricing made attorney services more widely available at the same time as popular interest in access to the courts created greater demand, and the resulting explosion in torts (lawsuits alleging damages between two parties) put huge pressure on the insurance market, forcing premium costs to rise while coverage shrank.

While liability issues were pressing down on the building industry — where missed schedules, blown budgets and various technical failures have always been rife — the wide availability of low-cost personal computers combined with desktop-based architectural design programs transformed the traditional methods of hand drafting to computer-aided design (CAD).

Computer-aided design (CAD)

Instruments of service began to transform accordingly. CAD-generated drawings, which actually simply substituted hand drawing for electronic plotting, gave the false appearance of great precision and accuracy, raising expectations on the parts of clients and contractors about the efficacy and competence of the authors. But nothing inherent in CAD made for more accurate drawings. At the same time, the ability to copy, enlarge and replicate chunks of graphics with CAD gave architects an exculpatory strategy: by drawing more, they hoped to shield themselves from accusations that their work was incomplete or inaccurate. Drawings sets exploded in size, often stretching into hundreds of sheets. Whether there was a commensurate increase in quality (or reduction in potential lawsuits) is a matter of debate. But there were a lot more lines on paper shown to describe a building designed by an architect.[34]

32 The advent of digital technology, according to David Barkin, State Architect of Connecticut, has caused a strange "technical inversion" of expertise, where supervising architects, while knowing well how a building goes together, don't understand the technology necessary to document it; their digitally savvy staff, just the opposite (personal correspondence with the author, July 2017).
33 Unfortunately, the US set an example for expanding liability in construction in other places in the world, including the UK and Australia, where lawsuits eventually became the remedy for failing projects and unresolved, increasingly contentious relationships.
34 "More lines on paper does not mean a commensurate increase in quality," according to Barkin.

2.3.1 An early BIM information display

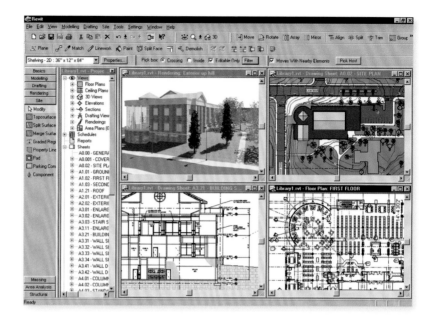

Ironically, the CAD era created the first important pressure on the concept of responsible control for licensed designers. In the pre-CAD age, the lead architect on a project (and the person who was ultimately putting her stamp on the drawings) might draw some of the set, but her team's work was easily on display as drawings taped to drafting boards being worked on in the open. A simple walk around the studio provided excellent insight into what was happening as a project was documented. And since hand-drawing elements of a project were both exacting and time-consuming to produce, those sets were carefully planned, monitored and controlled for quality. CAD took those same drawings, translated them into digital counterparts and locked them inside screens and hard drives, accessible only with software that the lead architect likely was unable to understand let alone actually use. Exercising responsible control moved from direct observation (or creation) of analog drawings to extracting plots from computers and reviewing paper proxies of the digital drawings. Consider this the first degree of separation from the original intent of the architect's responsible control.

Authority and digitization

As we now know, the advent of CAD was just the beginning of the widespread digitization of the design process. If CAD signaled the translation of hand drawing in two dimensions from paper to the paper space of AutoCAD, by 2005 another transformation was underway from CAD to building information modeling (BIM). Now not only are the project drawings locked in the

Building information modeling (BIM)

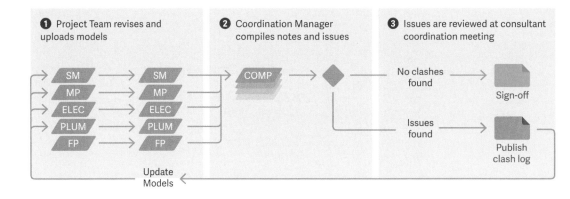

project server, they no longer even start out as drawings. The project is created as a digital twin in three dimensions, with data elements as proxies for building elements, and drawings are annotated reports from that database of elements. The resulting complexities of software interface and data management create further distance between the responsible controlling architect and the work itself — a second degree of separation. Information of similar complexity flows in from engineers, product manufacturers and other consultants. The architect remains on the hook for understanding, integrating and coordinating all this information in order to meet the basic requirements of both the standard of care and, by implication, maintaining responsible control. A taste of this information can be seen in Figure 2.3.1, an image from an early version of a popular building information modeling platform that displays how aspects of the project, all originating from a source database, can be displayed in three-dimensional, two-dimensional or textual form. A diagram of a strategy for organizing it across a team can be found in Figure 2.3.2.

2.3.1, 2.3.2

As we close out the second decade of the twenty-first century, BIM has become standard in many advanced construction economies,[35] but an expanded definition of responsible control lags behind, and the gap between that definition and evolving practice is not likely to close anytime soon, particularly as the next generation of technologies begins to appear in the design and construction process. If BIM created an information infrastructure for design and building — an epistemology of building configuration — the advent of faster computers and vast storage capacity (via the cloud) means even more computational power will be applied to the problems of design-

---

35 Jung and Lee, "The Status of Bim Adoption on Six Continents."

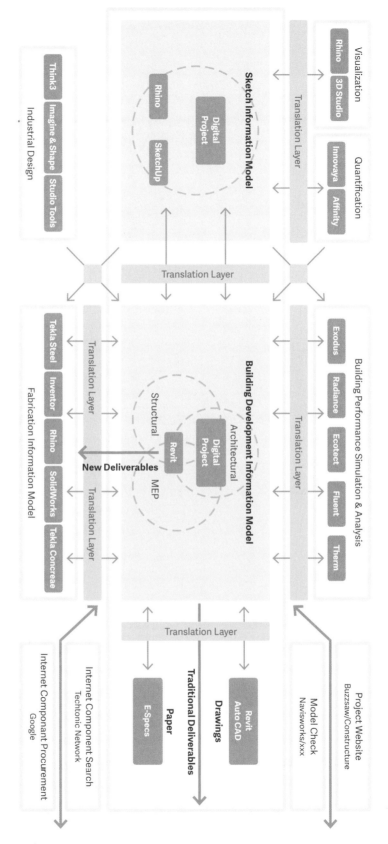

ing, building and operating. Big data, analytics, machine learning, outside data reference sources, robotics — these are all parts of the increasingly complex information structures of design and construction. The days of 'application-centric' projects, where most of the data on a job is created by a single 'hero' application ("this is a Revit project, or a Microstation project") will give way to an information inversion: the project comprises heterogeneous data from numerous programs and sources, and the applications that created that data are incidental to the overall project process. Design information, for example, as argued elsewhere in this text (see Chapter 3.5, "Design Demands of Digital Making"), is increasingly the basis for construction logic. Generative design scripting is becoming integral to design definition and output. Analytical software provides continuous monitoring of a design as it unfolds, and greatly expands opportunities for optimization. And delivery models themselves now include the participation, insight and even design deliverables from fabricators, contractors and building material providers. Figure 2.3.3 suggests that, even as BIM became a central tool for architects around 2007, multiple other applications were in use, generating data that needed coordination. Clearly, the original 'watching the pencils' construction of responsible control — and with it, the core responsibilities of the architect — must necessarily transform beyond NCARB's recognition.

2.3.3

New obligations for control circa 2007

The architect's responsibility for maintaining a coordinated, integrated view of the project should not depend on the platform used to create the instruments of service. In the analog and early CAD eras, the architect was the party responsible for finding and articulating that vision, given that drawings are orthographic projections of a three-dimensional phenomenon of building that otherwise does not exist except in her head. BIM is a platform where basic geometry and associated metadata such as quantities, materials and connections can be managed in 'real space'; it thereby transfers the obligation of geometric integration from the architect's brain to the computer's memory. The building itself, however, is far more complex than any BIM model can be; the design intent as defined in the now BIM-derived instruments of service does not reflect building function, code compliance, structural integrity, programmatic function, construction logic or even sufficient precision for building fabrication. Even as BIM has eased some of this burden, buildings themselves are complex in the era of sustainability, high-speed construction and digital fabrication. The tools are more robust, the relationships more complex, but the responsibility for some sort of next-generation responsible control remains.

If the intent of responsible control lies in assuring the public of competent building, there is a regulatory interest in refining — or at least understanding — the concept to respect new and emerging realities of digital design and construction. In today's challenging design and construction environment almost any exchange of information takes the form of a 'technical submission' submission, so we will stipulate that the regulatory desire for control and competency spans, both in a broad and deep way, across the entirety of the architect's responsibilities.

With this premise, two components of the NCARB definition of responsible control over the contents of the instruments of service bear closer scrutiny: first, the "control and detailed professional knowledge of the content... and its preparation" — in other words, the supervisory responsibility in the creation of the instruments of service; and second, the underlying understanding of the content itself. 'Professional knowledge' might be seen as an umbrella under which almost any competency would fit, but NCARB's construction of the phrase, specifically coupled with the obligation to understand 'content,' emphasizes the architect's obligation to understand the technical representation, depicted both graphically and in the specifications, as "written on the page" of the drawings. The architect with responsible control should understand the implications of a detail as drawn, a material as selected, the relationship of interconnected systems as specified by the architect and her consultants, and the myriad other co-dependent decisions that comprise a complex set of technical design documents and, by implication, the building they represent.

With respect to the instruments of service, there is a dramatic difference today in how the particular technical delineation eventually 'reaches the page' in a set of drawings, in contrast with CAD-based processes a decade ago. The ultimate set of decisions that result in a particular detail are a confluence of design intent from the architect, engineering objectives by consultants, material selections, specification, analytical processes that support the decisions, simulations and a myriad of other processes. So while NCARB's generalized description of the obligations of the responsible architect may be broad enough to carry this newly defined load, it is a dramatically larger load indeed.

The burden even increases with regard to the definition of 'content.' When the concept of responsible control originated in the pre-digital age, technical information of any sort delivered as an instrument of service by the architect was a relatively abstract, two-dimensional graphic representation of a partial extraction of a specific building view, such as the plan of the building shown in Figure 2.3.4. Such a view includes geometry, dimensions, annotations and in some cases additional metadata like notes or even references to the specification. It has relationships, by definition, to other parts of the technical representation of the building. The example shown here is a 'plan report' extracted from a BIM database that contains a comprehensive set of metadata including, for example, material quantities and three-dimensional relationships to other building components. As regards NCARB's intention for content, so far, so good. But if this particular plan is used, for ex-

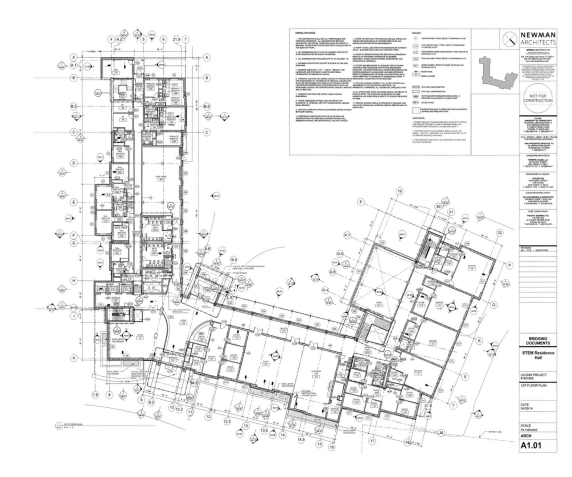

ample, as the basis of the construction strategy for the building, or contains additional representational information on behalf of the contractor, the scope of the architect's responsibility for the content is dramatically expanded. Information extracted from BIM databases, like the one that created this plan, is becoming the basis for fabrication of building elements (like windows, walls and doors). To the extent that such information transcends the design intent to also include, in the given example, the construction logic, the architect's responsibility for understanding, evaluating, integrating and ultimately approving the information — to wit, to exercise responsible control — expands dramatically.

One might argue that this expanding pressure on the responsibilities of the architect demands a regulatory response where the elements and scope of responsible control are redefined to reflect these new realities. I suspect that, given the open nature of its current definition, the standard of care will evolve pragmatically, project by project, as processes and procedures change to reflect new digital realities. The work of architects is subject to the relentless review of regulators, who hope to guide (but take no responsibility for) the results of design work. The evolution of the architect's responsible control must navigate between the demands of competent construction (for the client's benefit) and the public's health, safety and welfare. Today, these two questions are intertwined, to the confusion of all. And the analytical automation that soon will support the design process will likely eventually supplement — and then replace — human building officials and site inspectors with intelligent machines.

It is also possible to see the standard of care as a retardant to innovation in practice, in that it is essentially backward-looking and based on precedent. In order for the profession to move forward (and drag the standard along with it) practitioners must introduce innovations, implement them competently so as not to be accused of negligence, and hope over time the ideas permeate into typical practice. This is hardly a strategy for wholesale improvement in our — or any — professional discipline.

This highlights a related question apparent from those realities, an issue that may become a danger or an opportunity: the liability engendered by these enlarged obligations of the architect. History suggests that our profession, led too strongly by professional liability insurance companies, shirks that risk, and the industry is rife with cost estimators, construction managers, client representatives and other specialty consultants who have filled the breach. Will the next wave of such consultants be design and construction information integrators, or even algorithms? Yet this same situation offers an opportunity for new value creation that cannot be underestimated. By embracing these new responsibilities, architects can not only control and propel the development of good design, but also offer important, measurable and critical services to the building enterprise.

2.4

Preparing Digital Designers

As the integration of digital methods changes the nature of design processes and results, what is the appropriate definition of competency and how does it affect, if at all, professional education?

Up to this point I have argued for several seismic shifts in the roles and responsibilities of architects. So, what constitutes a competent architect as she enters mid-career, say in 2030, and how do we think about training to-day? Figure 2.4.1 is a roadmap, based on US education paths, showing when students at today's writing in 2018 might expect to graduate, become licensed, and reach mid-career no earlier than 2030.

2.4.1

Two different perspectives on professional competency can help frame this question. The first is capabilities: what does a competent architect need to be able to do to be a successful professional in this new context? Sadly, not only does the traditional definition of competence — the standard of care — provide little or no help, but actually retards an investigation of this question as it is a backward-looking frame. The reference to "what a competent architect in similar circumstances" would do used in the legal definition of proper professional performance is hardly helpful as it strongly privileges established practice, and that is certainly not where our architect working in 2030 needs to find herself. We need to project a new set of obligations for this future architect, based on both the opportunities and threats of new technologies and techniques, and then extrapolate the related competencies, from which in turn we might speculate on the obligations for professional education. As architects, we should design our way through this problem.

Computation and capabilities

This discussion cannot be complete today without looking carefully at a second set of influences entirely different from the opportunities of technology, to wit: the effects of automation on work in general and particularly, how increasing computational capabilities will pressure the professions. In the emergent era of autonomous cars, ubiquitous data and computers that can learn and reason, what might architects worry about and what strategies are available to respond accordingly? If computers are increasingly able to do

	2018	2019	2020	2021	2022	2023	2024	2025	2026	2027	2028	2029	2030	2031	2032	2033	2034	2035	2036	2037	2038
High School Student	Finishes high school	B. Arch (5)					Professional Experience + Test					License	Early mid-career								
4 year Bachelors	Finishes B.A / B.S	Work experience		Grad School			Professional Experience + Test						License	Early mid-career							
B. Arch	Finishes B. Arch		Professional Experience + Test				License	Early mid-career													
M. Arch	Finishes M. Arch	Professional Experience + Test				License	Early mid-career														

things that were once only the province of architects, how does competency change? And how should the profession position itself in this constellation of automated processes and capabilities?

Let us stipulate that the future practice of architecture (from now until 2030) retains the fundamental characteristics established by Alberti: that society still requires a professional to mediate its aesthetic, technical and legal needs for building. While it may be in some way feasible to completely either automate and/or outsource the design of a building and not involve humans on the ground at or near the project site, it seems unlikely that clients or regulators (like building departments) will be comfortable assigning responsibility to disembodied algorithms even if they are BIM-enabled. The signature and seal on a set of drawings still signifies personal responsibility for the design. Furthermore, although the architect may find herself in a different position relative to the activities of construction, buildings will continue to be complex and technically challenging to create, and the three key roles — client, designer and builder — will persist.

Each of these players comes to the building process with fundamentally different objectives, which they hope will mesh and result in a successful building. The client aspires to have a project that fulfills its expectations (for beauty, functionality, performance, price and schedule) by enlisting the architect to translate those desires into an articulation of design intent that is suitable for a builder to execute. In this sense, the architect is the bridge between aspiration and execution, and her capabilities must satisfy the demands generated by both client and builder.

Aspiration, intent, execution

Technology's progress in 2030

Technologies and related processes will certainly have evolved significantly by 2030, but let us set out the following assumptions from which to speculate about the related capabilities of the architect:

— **Modeling** Digital modeling, and particularly the successors to BIM-based systems, are fully mature and capable of high-resolution representations of building materials, behaviors and construction techniques.
— **Prediction** Those models are augmented by computationally robust analytical systems that can rapidly evaluate the results of design and construction decisions across a wide range of issues, from the prosaic (cost, schedule, energy consumption) to the more exotic (occupant behavior and health, building lifecycle, fire and life safety protection, construction methodology).
— **Generation** Drawing, modeling and direct manipulation of a design representation will remain central methodologies, but they will be augmented by algorithms that generate an array of potential alternatives for examination.
— **Big data** Industry players have aggregated large 'data lakes' of information gathered from design information (models, analysis) and actual conditions (construction data, sensor inputs from operating buildings). These data have been exhaustively examined by machine learning algorithms.
— **Collaboration** Various software tools and digital design and constructability capabilities have been integrated in interoperable, transparent collaboration platforms making data easy to generate, distribute, and integrate into other processes. This data infrastructure forms the basis of collaboration strategies for projects.
— **Industrialized building** Construction sites and processes are more automated and industrialized, and more components of buildings are fabricated off-site and assembled on site rather than being built *in situ* by hand-based craft.

Practice competencies in 2030

Practice Analysis of Architecture

In the US, NCARB researches the competencies demanded of architects by extensively surveying the profession.[36] Their 2012 *Practice Analysis of Architecture*[37] identified over one hundred knowledge or skill areas that an architect must master to achieve the minimal competency of licensure. Even if understanding how the technologies discussed above might affect this lengthy architectural 'to-do list' is beyond the scope of this exploration, there

36 The National Council of Architectural Registration Boards, a consortium of boards of licensing who regulate the practice of architecture in individual US States.
37 National Council of Architectural Registration Boards (NCARB) (ed.), *2012 Ncarb National Practice Analysis of Architecture* (Washington, DC: NCARB, 2012). See https://www.ncarb.org/sites/default/files/2013PA_BoxSet_AllReports.pdf.

EDU TASK #	Additional tasks identified as "not introduced" in education by interns who completed IDP within the past two years, and architects licensed in the past year (listed from highest to lowest)
86	Establish procedures for building commissioning.
91	Determine billing rates.
54	Determine specific insurance requirements to meet contract or business needs.
80	Review application and certificate for payment.
56	Manage modifications to the construction contract.
69	Negotiate terms and conditions of services outlined in architect-consultant agreement.
68	Establish procedures for providing post-occupancy services.
90	Develop strategies to control risk and manage liability.
92	Develop business plan for firm.
79	Coordinate testing of building performance and materials.
53	Establish procedures to process documentation during contract administration.
62	Negotiate terms and conditions outlined in owner-architect agreement.
85	Manage project-specific bidding process.
71	Establish procedures for documenting project decisions.
74	Manage client expectations to align with established milestones and final decision points.
87	Select design team consultants.
95	Develop procedures for responding to contractor requests (requests for information).
8	Evaluate results of feasibility studies to determine project's financial viability.
59	Prepare proposals for services in response to client requirements.
6	Determine design fees.
96	Develop strategies for responding to owner requests (requests for proposal, requests for qualifications).
77	Identify changes in project scope that require additional services.
83	Manage information exchange during construction.
50	Perform constructability review to determine ability to procure, sequence construction, and build proposed project.
94	Develop procedures for responding to changes in project scope.
89	Participate in pre-constuction, pre-installation, and regular progress meeting with design team.
58	Respond to contractor requests for information.
51	Perform constructability reviews throughout the design process.
78	Assist owner in obtaining necessary permits and approvals.
57	Prepare owner-contractor agreement.
81	Review shop drawings and submittals during construction for conformance with design intent.
76	Manage implementation of sustainability criteria.
49	Prepare life cycle cost analysis.
52	Prepare final procurement and contract documents.
61	Prepare architect-consultant agreement.

are at least four general areas of competence that our 2030 practitioner will
need to achieve (beyond the basics established in the current standards of

licensure):

1. Design validation Design will always be a fundamental value delivered by
architects: the ability to take numerous ambiguous inputs, analyze opportunities, generate alternative solutions and work with a client to explore, lo-
cate and actualize a solution to a building challenge. And the design process
will always require the sort of heuristic reasoning described by Peter Rowe
and Horst Rittel (see Chapter 2.1, "The Digital Transformation of Design");
building design will always be a 'wicked problem.' What is likely to change is
not the basics of design methodology but rather the inputs that constrain it
and the processes of validation necessary to make the case for a given design. The relatively new inputs will originate from three sources.

First, modeling tools will improve to the point where the building can
be represented at arbitrary levels of abstraction, from simple proxies ("I need
a wall here, but I don't know how thick it is or even what it is made out of.") to
detailed, performance-based systems that include instructions for assembly
("This is a pre-fabricated wall manufactured by Company X, which costs this
much, requires this much time to install, and the installation procedure looks
like this."). An architect using such a tool can choose what information might
be relevant to the particular problem she is trying to solve and adjust the
resulting representation for its use.

Second, connecting the parameters inherent in the model representation of the design as it evolves to algorithms, which are emerging from today's scripting tools like Grasshopper or Dynamo, allows our designer to generate design alternatives computationally. Adjusting the various parametric
inputs of the model controlled by the algorithm allows the designer to create
far more such alternatives than could be created by a human alone.

Finally, analytical results will evaluate, in close to real time, the implications of design decisions as they are generated. Structural engineers have
used such tools for years, which relieves them of the burdens of iterative
computations of structural systems. Those capabilities will extend to a broad
range of evaluations, limited only by our ability to create the necessary analytical strategies and resulting simulations. Simulation results will be augmented by insights yielded by big data collected from originating design
models, construction site documentation and building operational data.

Thus the obligation to define and execute a design exploration in a
way that can be understood and validated augments the architect's responsibility in creating the design intent. While the ethos of the "brilliant napkin
sketch," an outcome of the best sort of heuristic thinking, will likely never
disappear, those flashes of insight will need to be substantiated with analysis that demonstrates — particularly to the other players like clients, build-

ers, regulators — that the resulting ideas actually work. The napkin sketch of the future may well contain an idea for a script that creates the form, rather than the object itself.

For generations architects have been trained to generate and document formal architectural ideas while understanding and integrating technical and performance requirements in the service of accomplishing those forms.[38] Formal considerations will likely remain at the top of the design education hierarchy, but tomorrow's designers will need to learn to marshal form-generating and form-validating tools in concert. Even more synthetic thinking and architectural judgment will be necessary to sort through, evaluate and select appropriate solutions. Most important, digitally empowered designers must not fall prey to the trap described (see Preface) by the architect Cesar Pelli: do not use the computer for 'the systematic generation of useless alternatives,' as doing so gives precisely the opposite result to what a validated design process makes possible.

2. Information integration and coordination We should assume that the same set of tools that empower our architect in 2030 will be available in various forms to her collaborators, whose instruments of service will be comprised of various digital models, text and simulations. The architect has always had, in many countries, an obligation to make sure that the information coming from her sub-consultants is properly integrated into the overall instruments of service for the project. The American Institute of Architects memorialized this obligation in a standard form of agreement for the Architect as follows:

> *Consistent with its Standard of Care, Architect shall be responsible for the accuracy and coordination of all drawings and design documents relating to Architect's design and used on the Project, regardless of whether such drawings and documents are prepared or performed by Architect, or by Architect's consultants, including, without limitation, the drawings and specifications prepared by the Civil Engineer, Structural Engineer, Mechanical, Electrical and Plumbing Engineer, and Landscape Architect. Consistent with its Standard of Care, Architect shall be responsible for coordination and internal checking of all drawings and for the accuracy of all dimensional and layout information contained in the drawings and specifications prepared by Architect's consultants, as fully as if each drawing were prepared by Architect.[39]*

38 One of my engineering instructors in graduate school exclaimed, "I'm not trying to turn you into a structural engineer. I'm trying to teach you how to work with one."
39 American Institute of Architects, Standard Form of Owner Architect B101-2007, Section 3.2.7.

The paragraph describes in practical terms (relative to when it was written, before 2007) the architect's duty to make sure that the instruments of service coalesce properly into a coherent project in a traditional process of analog, paper-based graphical drawings that should have 'dimensional accuracy.' As we near the year 2020, there are a myriad of tools that organize, distribute and monitor the digital counterparts of such analog drawings (solutions like Autodesk's BIM360, Bentley's ProjectWise or their competitors). These platforms structure information, maintain version control, store it in a central location and distribute it widely via the internet to dispersed teams, and assure that model-based information is properly synchronized for multiple users.

By 2030, however, the challenges of design integration will multiply by virtue of not simply the increasing amount of data, but rather the growing complexity and interconnectivity of decisions being made by multiple consultants. At one level, this is clearly a technical challenge that we can be confident is a large enough commercial opportunity that the software vendors will attack and solve it.[40] In that sense, technical coordination and checking is likely to be automated and less of a challenge.

Orchestrating a design team empowered by such tools is a different proposition, however, particularly given the singular nature of today's design training where, in the design studio, the solitary author reigns king. If our assumptions about the complex web of information and validation that will comprise the 2030 design process is correct, that particular orchestra needs a conductor to prevent total cacophony, and the architect should take that role in the service of assuring that her design intent is fully realized. The technical particulars of such a role — different types of software, hardware, networking and data structures — are far less important than the ability to plan, coordinate and manage a complex team of collaborators toward best results. This suggests that our architect in 2030 might benefit as much from leadership and collaboration training, not unlike what her school counterparts in the MBA program experience.[41]

3. Design-to-construction continuity The division of labor between intent and execution — between the architect and the contractor — is the source of much frustration and inefficiency, usually wrought to the detriment of the client and the project. Profit margins, risk management and insurance constraints, construction worker injuries, and just a lack of mutual understand-

---

40 Autodesk's research project Quantum purports to do just that, by providing an integrated work environment that connects software, data and versioning in a single, integrated location.

41 For the past eight years we have taught a leadership, decision-making and collaboration curriculum at Yale School of Architecture during the First Year Building Project that is designed to acquaint architectural students with the basic concepts of working in teams. We combine exercises, assessment tools and lectures to demonstrate that teamwork is an acquired skill as well as a discipline necessary for design leadership.

2.4.3 Architecture students from Yale assembling a digitally fabricated house in 2017

ing across the intent-execution gap are some of the underlying reasons for the distance between design and construction. However, there are several forces at work, likely to be in full play by 2030, drawing architects and contractors together.

First and foremost, digital information that originates during design is very useful to the contractor during construction. In a paper-based world, the builder must carefully read, interpret and often transcribe and redraw information from the architect to be in a form suitable for bidding, procurement, fabrication or assembly. The most common form of this translation is shop drawings, but (as described in Chapter 2.2, "Defining Design Intent: Depiction, Precision and Generation") the architect's primary responsibility is to define intent and let the contractor figure out what that might mean and how to make it happen. Working together (and with the appropriate business arrangements, discussed in Chapter 3.3, "Designing Design: Optimizing, Solving, Selecting"), the architect can organize and deliver information that is useful to both herself and the builder, while eliminating inefficient steps in today's process.

As construction moves inexorably toward more modern techniques more typical of manufacturing, digital information originated by the architect is not just helpful but necessary. The general trend of 'industrial construction' — prefabricated components and automated/robotic-assisted construction techniques are two examples — creates an enormous demand for data that can feed the machines that build. To the extent that those techniques are perfected, they will create libraries of assembly methodologies that can loop back into the originating design processes themselves, in a virtuous cycle that improves design and thereby its results. The 'execution gap' narrows, efficiency improves, and results become more predictable.

Architects and builders radically differ on how insightful the former is about the latter's work and vice versa. Architects claim that effective design is impossible without involvement in construction, and in the US, 25% of the architect's fee is typically allocated to working during that phase of a project.[42] Builders, on the other hand, citing challenging construction documents produced by architects and arms-length relationships on the job site, suggest that architects have much to learn about construction[43]. Most architecture programs today contain some provision for training in construction[44] but those experiences are more likely to involve swinging hammers and pouring concrete than planning and executing a digitally fabricated building. Today's students should become familiar with digital fabrication at building scale (far beyond, say, 3D printing) and develop an understanding of how digital design information transits from design intent, through purchase and fabrication, to the job site for assembly.

2.4.3

4. Data aggregation and analysis Architectural training today owes more to the tradition of the École des Beaux-Arts than to the Bauhaus, privileging design as an aesthetic and artistic rather than a technical endeavor. One consequence of this priority is that architectural design as a practice suffers from the resulting lack of empirical, evidence-based knowledge that will be a critical component of design in 2030.

Emerging interest in computation has paralleled that of research as a discipline in firms. Many firms today purport to do 'research' in some form, but others like Kieran Timberlake instantiate it into daily practice, including professionally trained researchers (some of whom are also architects) in their typical design strategies and methodologies. This trend will continue as computers demand the rationalization of design approaches both consuming and generating swaths of data along the way.

Ubiquitous computational power delivered to any point of work via cloud and mobile technologies means that enormous amounts of data can

42 This is the typical allocation of the architect's fee during construction on an American project. Practice standards vary wildly across the world, from Brazil (where the architect has no role whatsoever during construction) to Japan, where the architect's services are provided as part of the cost of construction when the project is built by a large general contractor. These Japanese firms often have hundreds of architects on staff to do this work.
43 Harvey M. Bernstein, "Managing Uncertainty and Expectations in Building Design and Construction."
44 Students at the Yale School of Architecture participate in the First Year Building Project where they design and build a building from start to finish, a part of a curriculum originated by Dean Charles Moore fifty years ago. It was only in 2017 that those students began extensive offsite fabrication of building components.

	Technology/Process						Obligation	Competency	Pedagogy
	Modeling	*Prediction*	*Generation*	*Big data*	*Collaboration*	*Industrialized building*			
❶ Design validation	●	●	●	●			Demonstrate outcomes of design	Integrate analytical results with design strategy	Deploy analysis is service of heuristics
❷ Information integration and coordination	●	●		●	●	●	Coordinate all digital project information to service project	Organize and prioritize collaboration approaches	Manage team dynamics
❸ Design-to-construction continuity	●	●	●			●	Bridge design information to assist in construction	Understand construction implications of design decisions	Design to build
❹ Data aggregation and analysis		●	●	●			Leverage big data sources to support design and construction outcomes	Structure, collect, manage data and systems	Understand building data epistemology

be collected, evaluated, interpreted, and redistributed in just about any context. Google, Amazon, Netflix, and most hospitals collect and use such data today, and as design and construction are increasingly digitized a similar opportunity can be leveraged. In fact, as modern business in general becomes more dependent on big data and evidence to drive decisions, similar validation of the architect's design recommendations will be expected by clients. Architects designing projects for Google are already working this way, consistent with the world view of their clients.[45]

Our architect in 2030 will live in a world where enormous data sets are easily collected, analyzed and leveraged to her advantage. Those data lakes might be collections of design and analysis models from previous projects, digital recordings and data from construction projects, user data from building use or telemetry collected from automated building management systems. Machine learning algorithms will search and evaluate this data, returning conclusions about the efficacy of design decisions on constructability and building function.

Much like today's BIM managers, the technical implementation and management of big data systems will likely be left to specialists, or perhaps The Mas-

---

45 Paul Goldberger, "Google's New Built-from-Scratch Googleplex," *Vanity Fair* (2013), https://www.vanityfair.com/news/tech/2013/02/exclusive-preview-googleplex.

The Master Algorithm[46] that learns how to learn from lots of data. For the architect, however, it will be important to understand the sources, uses and organization of data that can support her design process. Much like the research training that traditional academics receive before writing a thesis, we'll need to train architects to collect evidence that can both help validate design outcomes and add to the body of knowledge of the industry itself.

2.4.4

The future of the professions

Today's architects are buffeted by the winds of change in project delivery and liability. Architects in 2030 will similarly not be in complete control of their professional destinies, but for a different set of reasons. Just as technology has disrupted work since the first industrial revolution, the Second Machine Age[47] will change professional practice across many disciplines, and architecture in particular. An exploration — in equal parts fascinating and terrifying — of this question is presented by the father/son team from Oxford of Richard and Daniel Susskind in their recent book *The Future of the Professions*.[48] The Susskinds predict the ultimate demise of professions as we know them today, eliminated by the emergence of para-professionals, digitally embedded and accessible knowledge, and machine-provided expertise. Like textile workers of the eighteenth century replaced by automated looms, large swaths of professional expertise and knowledge will be automated and their previous gatekeepers — lawyers, doctors, architects — will no longer control it, all of which will allegedly provide society with higher levels of service at lower costs. And they cite the productivity of BIM as a reason for diminished demand for architects.[49] Like me and my long-lost CAD and hand drafting abilities, the architects who remain will be 'deskilled' by computers doing large parts of their jobs.

A similar argument is offered by Babson professor Thomas Davenport and his Harvard collaborator Julia Kirby in *Only Humans Need Apply: Winners and Losers in the Age of Smart Machine*.[50] Rather than suggesting that entire professions will be destroyed by automation, they argue for what they call 'augmentation' through automation, and counsel today's workers to look for opportunities to accelerate their human-only skills (like synthetic reasoning, human relations, persuasion) with computer-supported processes that machines do best. And they quote an encouraging 2013 study that seems to suggest that architects may be somewhat protected from the creative de-

46 Pedro Domingos, *The Master Algorithm: How the Quest for the Ultimate Learning Machine Will Remake Our World* (New York: Basic Books, 2015).

47 Brynjolfsson and McAfee, *The Second Machine Age: Work, Progress, and Prosperity in a Time of Brilliant Technologies.*

48 Richard E. Susskind and Daniel Susskind, *The Future of the Professions: How Technology Will Transform the Work of Human Experts,* (Oxford, UK: Oxford University Press, 2015).

49 Although it is important that, as of this writing in 2018, demand for architects, fee volume and employment levels for architects are surging. Kermit Baker, "How Many Architects Does Our Economy Need?," *ARCHITECT* (05 January 2018).

50 *Thomas H. Davenport and Julia Kirby, Only Humans Need Apply: Winners and Losers in the Age of Smart Machines,* (New York: Harper Business, 2016).

struction of automation because "(o)ccupations that involve complex perception and manipulation tasks, creative intelligence tasks, and social intelligence tasks are unlikely to be substituted by computer capital over the next decade or two."[51]

The most 'wicked' aspects of practice surely fall within these boundaries, even if many of the more 'tame' tasks do not, and are likely to be automated as a result. But Davenport and Kirby recommend a series of strategies for today's knowledge workers to achieve augmentation, of which the most relevant to architects is what they call 'stepping up,' a three-part approach where architects could explicitly decide how automation will augment design processes, create new, effective workflows where humans and machines collaborate, and then constantly monitor and improve the results.

Architects must thus apply their skills as designers to create an 'augmented, automated' future for our discipline, lest the inexorable forces described by the Susskinds overwhelm the profession altogether. A careful consideration of its larger objectives — including social, aesthetic and technical outcomes — should govern a re-examination of how architects design, collaborate, and relate to construction while taking full advantage of the powerful capabilities of new technologies. We must generate a clear strategy for the future of practice and marshal all our intellectual resources accordingly. The academy and the regulators of licensure have central roles: the academy can define a theoretical platform for architectural relevance while creating new methods and workflows for design, as the regulators of architectural practice redefine competency in the digital age. Our architect of 2030 will thus be properly trained to keep architecture — and architects — relevant, capable and empowered.

51 Carl Benedikt Frey, Michael A. Osborne, "The Future of Employment: How Susceptible Are Jobs to Computerization" (2013), https://www.oxfordmartin.ox.ac.uk/downloads/academic/The_Future_of_Employment.pdf.

2.5

Building Performance Design

How do evolving social expectations of building — like urbanism or sustainability — change the inherent expectations of design results and the architect's role?

Society can only evolve as a simultaneous ordering and articulation of space. The elaboration of the built environment, however haphazard, precarious and based on accident, rather than purpose and intention, originally, seems to be a necessary condition for the build-up of any stable social order. The gradual build-up of a social system must go hand in hand with the gradual build-up of an artificial spatial order. Social order therefore requires spatial order. The social process needs the built environment as a plane of inscription, where it can leave traces that then serve to build up and stabilize social structures that then in turn allow a further elaboration of more complex social processes.
Patrik Schumacher, Zaha Hadid Architects[52]

At their best, architects create direct, functional, and beautiful buildings that engage their larger context to create something more than merely a structure, but a vitally important and contributing piece of a larger framework.
Paul Mankins, American Institute of Architects[53]

What is the value of design, and designers?

As the architectural profession rose from the ashes of the 2008 worldwide economic crisis, the American Institute of Architects embarked upon a marketing campaign, having concluded that the best thing for America's architects (as many as 30% of whom were unemployed) was to equip them with messages to declare, once again, the value of architects and architecture.

52 Patrik Schumacher, Vienna IOA Silver Lecture, 2011, as transcribed at http://www.patrikschumacher.com/Texts/The%20Societal%20Function%20of%20Architecture.html, quoting from his book *The Autopoiesis of Architecture.*
53 American Institute of Architects (ed.), "The Architect's Voice: Advocating for Our Profession," in *AIA* (Washington, DC, 2016), p. 19.

Collateral from that campaign includes the so-called *Architect's Message Book*,[54] a compendium of ideas and quotes to assure clients of the importance and role of architects in the built environment and society. The section called "Architects strengthen society" offers the following headlines relevant to their contribution:

— Architects are a vital component of all design/build and community projects.
— We add value and provide solutions in a variety of ways.
— Architects build communities with a focus on sustainable outcomes.
— Design has always been crucial to people's lives but now it plays a greater role than ever before.
— We are vital community partners who provide valuable skills and services.
— Great design is necessary for a healthy community.[55]

"Parametricism"

Around that same time, Patrik Schumacher, director of Zaha Hadid Architects and a leading digital architect, proposed a new architectural style, "Parametricism," which purportedly left formalistic conceits behind for the procedural possibilities of computationally driven architecture. He declared that the architectural 'orders' in the aftermath of the economic crisis are scripted procedures creating infinitely variable forms that respond not so much to aesthetic but functional demands of spatial use. Shape and material do not comprise the Parametricist style, but rather the constraints, influences and combinations of process and vectors that shape space and form itself. Form follows function, but now function is a broad interpretation of the social and technical influences that shape space, controlled by the architect's algorithms that represent them. Here automation doesn't simply augment the capabilities of the designer but rather transforms them entirely.

Although it may be unfair to compare AIA's marketing gibberish with Parametricism theory, both Mankins and Schumacher apparently see the role of architects in somewhat different lights, although both parties probably agree that good buildings are both functional and beautiful. Either way, professional architects design a very small percentage of the world's buildings, so somehow their respective value propositions have little traction with everyday clients who commission those projects and largely elect to build without the services of said architects.

The social value of design

Perhaps society sees architects as either artistic and unnecessary, or worse, relies on engineers and builders for the most important technical questions,

54 Ibid.
55 Ibid., p. 29.

2.5.1 Proposal model for
Brunelleschi's dome over the
Duomo, Florence

2.5.2 Interior of Guangzhou Opera House by Zaha Hadid Architects

separating the functional from the aesthetic. Schumacher suggests that this is a false binary, and that architecture itself is autopoietic,[56] self-contained and self-referential in a system that combines and relies upon both the expressive and the technical. He does not mean that architects operate autonomously, creating objects without reference or reliance on outside systems or influences (like, for example, artists or even engineers), but rather the discipline itself rises to the level of what he calls a "modern functional system," similar to politics, law or medicine, with its own theoretical platforms, methodologies, knowledge systems and standards. As such, architecture, as a means for creating the places of social existence, is a central ordering principle of society itself. Referring again to Alberti, who first posited the need for a non-technical, theoretical basis for design as a system of ideas independent of construction, Schumacher argues that humanity "escapes the animal kingdom" by refining social and spatial orders simultaneously, while at the same time creating "inscriptions of social memory" in those spaces via design.[57] Like philosophy, law or politics, architecture is an important means for society to find its way in the world. The technical requirements and the ineffable aspirations of building are thus inexorably intertwined.

The ability to represent and explore abstract ideas about building before committing to actual construction began with the first designers using images in the shape of drawings or models. Brunelleschi convinced his cli-

56 An autopoietic system is one that is capable of reproducing and sustaining itself (see https://en.wikipedia.org/wiki/ Poiesis).
57 Schumacher, Vienna IOA Silver Lecture.

2.5.1

ents in Florence to allow him to build the dome over Santa Maria del Fiore with a simple wooden model, as shown in Figure 2.5.1. As buildings and the systems of construction became increasingly complex (in parallel with social demands and capabilities) the means of representation evolved in concert. Just as Alberti separated the role of the architect from that of the constructor, the disciplines necessary to design and construct a building have been similarly elaborated. A complex building today — and the drawing set generated to achieve it — can be comprised of dozens of different disciplines ranging from the typical (structural engineering) to the esoteric (wayfinding, lighting design, security systems). Schumacher would argue that this explosion in the number of specialists necessary to design a building reflects our society's attempt to spatialize experience itself, but he would not call the technical elaboration of building 'architecture.' Those aspects of design and building are necessary but not sufficient to make architecture; the expression of social aspiration, behavior, process and interaction is the result of design and the generative force of architecture writ large, a force sup-

2.5.2

ported by its technical articulation.

Parametricism would seem, therefore, to lay excellent theoretical groundwork for the work of architects in the Second Machine Age, creating a rationale for a design methodology dependent on computation and measuring the results as how well the design meets fundamental social needs. While Schumacher makes the original case with a limited realm of computational simulations ("… [Parametricism] is the only style congenial to recent advances in structural and environmental engineering capacities based on computational analytics and optimization techniques"[58]) and an obsessive reliance on scripted geometry of generative tools like Grasshopper, the essential assertion remains correct: the norms and objectives established by society as expectations of its buildings will be increasingly encoded, like many aspects of "modern functional systems," in computational form. Structural and environmental requirements are just the tip of this simulative iceberg, and a logical point for Schumacher to start with the tools available around 2005. But, with those problems solved, now what?

This book argues for an extension of the notion of Parametricism to include not just the computational inputs to design but a reliance upon — and willingness to commit to — the outputs (the functional and social results of design), and in this way round out the compact between architects who design buildings and members of society who build and use them. The iterative design feedback loop inherent in a 'parametricist' design process of depiction, prediction and generation extends across construction to

---

58 Patrik Schumacher, *In Defense of Parametricism* (London, 2015; published by Machine Books in 2016 in the series "Styles: In Defense of…", edited by Austin Williams), http://www.patrikschumacher.com/Texts/In%20Defense%20of%20 Parametricism.html.

2.5.3 Computational fluid dynamics simulation of building airflow

2.5.4 Augmented reality design simulation

use. If buildings are created not as architecture *per se* but rather as a means to a social end (where schools educate, hospitals heal) there is great value in defining those objectives as explicit goals of the architect's services. Let us examine three categories of inputs and outputs that progress from today's technologies (like BIM, analytical algorithms and scripted optimization enabled in the future by big data, machine learning and expert systems) and then speculate on how this evolution might change the architect's value, both given and received.

Scripting, accelerated

While almost every architecture graduate today is a skilled scripter of geometry, BIM-enabled architects have a much broader array of parameters as inputs to a design solution, and a slowly expanding arsenal of accompanying analytical tools. Optimizing structure, airflow, or daylight as 'inputs' to solve discrete problems is well understood, and this first wave of analytics is based on the 'rules of design' established by the relevant technical disciplines. Testing a range of structural options or tracing the path of the sun through a piece of digital glass requires lots of computing cycles but limited data, and can thus be run on today's desktop computers. These are first-order 'social mandates' in the sense that they instantiate the requirements that buildings stand up and operate with environmental responsibility. In this case, computers augment the architect's capabilities to comply with building codes, which are at root social standards for building effectiveness. And in that sense, the demands of compliance and associated rules (and punishments) remain within the 'modern functional system' of architecture itself.

Simulation displayed

As desktop computers become faster, cheaper and, more importantly, connected to the cloud, another array of analytical tools will emerge to manipulate the parameters of design. Simulations that require large swaths of data managed with extensive computation will emerge and take on a second generation of objectives: cost estimating, construction simulation and basic occupancy evaluations, like "how many people fit in this lobby?" or "how long does it take everyone to escape this building in a fire?". These objectives are more performance-based than simple formula calculations, and include the dimension of time. Schumacher further asserts that each of these objectives should be solved in concert through computational representations that can make them connected, interdependent and evaluated in relationship to each

2.5.3, 2.5.4 other. The design strategy is more complicated, but the solutions are richer.

These richer solutions are important for reasons beyond the technical. In order to deliver real value to society, the functional systems of architecture (design and construction) must connect and make commitments to other adjacent systems upon which it depends: global finance (for capital), politics (for regulatory control) and law (for arbitraging risk). Each of those systems has begun to develop its own computational infrastructure to support its processes. Capital flows are arbitraged, speculated and managed through completely automated means, and risk assessment for the assignment of capital depends on big-data-based evaluations. If a common car loan can be reviewed and approved with an expert system, surely the ability to do the same for a construction loan or building bond issue cannot be far behind. Political jurisdictions have begun to collect data on utility systems, policing outcomes, traffic control, sanitation patterns and property ownership and are using that data to evaluate planning and operational strategies. And in an intersection of political and legal systems, Singapore has automated the process of submitting, reviewing and approving building permits.[59] If BIM is a knowledge platform from which outcome-based design can spring, it can also bridge the gaps between systems and their representations and thereby address social demands more directly. Architects can then project — and commit to — a different and important set of building objectives that reflect a higher social order, the best sort of augmentation of the architect's power.

This next generation of analytical platforms offers opportunities along on still another axis. At the intersection of urbanism and sustainability is the question of a building's relationship to the various scales within which it operates — from its site, through the neighborhood, to the city and the planet. Design and regulation of building today rarely reach beyond the systemic implications of water and energy use or traffic. Those characteristics

Scales of representation (and many others) ripple across the various scales of socially occupied space, but there are few means to understand, demonstrate or even constrain the implications of building. As digitized political and economic mod-

59 For further information on Singapore's automated system for permitting called CORENET see Singapore Building Construction Authority, "About Corenet" (2013), https://www.bca.gov.sg/newsroom/others/pr31102013_BCAA.pdf.

els become more robust and accessible, it will be possible to simulate the effects of buildings on all of them through interconnected systems of simulation.[60]

A current but challenging example of this opportunity can be found in the interest in carbon and its implications on global climate change. Today, a building's carbon footprint is derived largely from its lifetime use of energy, only exceptionally from the embodied energy and carbon in a given building subsystem, such as concrete (which is known to be inexpensive but incredibly carbon-intensive). The entire process of making a building, however, has many carbon-entangled tentacles that include the selection, manufacturing, delivery and installation of its various elements, the energy expended in preparing the site, and carbon is necessary to energize, repair and maintain and eventually demolish it. Socio-political structures that govern building have no means to understand these implications for a given project, or even consider its impacts outside of its own borders. If the configuration of space is proxy for a complex social process, the connection of the building to the global ecosystem has a similar relationship. Other functional systems willing, computation can enable an understanding of these broader implications and, in time, optimize them.[61]

Figure 2.5.4 sketches a simple example of this idea, looking at the interconnection of carbon impact from the scale of an individual building component — a sheet of glass in a curtainwall — through the component system, building, site, region, economy and eventually the globe. Chained systems of simulation and analysis will eventually enable designers to see, understand and design in these multiple contexts.

Analyzing experience Although Schumacher disdains the distinction between the two, a final realm of computational projection is experience and expression itself. While we may never have a time when a machine can discern the meaning of a building (a terrifying, and likely unreachable, capability of an algorithm) we certainly have the means today, through one of the most accessible techniques of simulation, to understand the dimensions and other physical qualities of spaces and their use before they are built. Virtual reality — the ability to visualize and experience spatial simulations — is already moving from viewing to interaction, and soon will include the advantages of augmented reality, where informational overlays on the visual field can provide even more insight directly in three-dimensional context. Again, this may be an issue of design inputs and performance outputs, because at the same time that we can simu-

(margin notes: Carbon footprint; 2.5.4; Virtual reality)

---

60 For further discussion of systems boundaries, see essays by Faircloth and Moe in Phillip G. Bernstein et al, *Goat Rodeo: Practicing Built Environments* (2015).
61 An example of this sort of integration can be found in Kieran Timberlake's TALLY BIM tool that measures life cycle cost implications of an emergent design. See https://kierantimberlake.com/pages/view/95/tally/parent:4.

scale	building component	building	neighborhood	region	planet
analysis					
cost	component cost ●	building cost ● →	○	○	○
economics	○	supply ●	labor availability ● →	economic perf ● →	GOP ●
energy	thermal perform ●	systems perform ● →	utility demand ● →	component cost ● →	renewables ●
traffic	○	demand ●	supply ● →	component cost ● →	○
carbon	○	generated, embodied ●	component cost ● →	climate change ● →	climate change ●

late the experience of a building, we can collect data on an occupant's reaction to it. There are plenty of immediate issues that such technologies could address, falling mainly in the realm of "does this space really work the way we want it to?". But over time, our understanding of the neurological basis of the perception of beauty may intersect with our ability to collect, evaluate and integrate the results with design strategies themselves. Data scientists are already studying the common characteristics of what observers find 'beautiful' in paintings and photographs in order to extract the principal characteristics.[62] The expressive power of a building may soon no longer be reduced, as it often is, to an argument between an architect and a planning board; computation might provide an aesthetic referee.

This is all to say that society as a whole, as argued by the Susskinds[63] and others, is moving itself toward the instantiation of desires, goals and standards that might be expressed computationally. This is hardly a threat but rather an enormous opportunity for architects. If the remit of architects has been shrinking in the last half-century in the face of insurance carriers, aggressive builders and insecure clients, the Second Machine Age is a chance to reverse the polarity of the equation. Design iteration, augmented

---

62 For a particularly creepy example of this challenge, where a machine learning algorithm learned to recognize the faces of cats and then took a turn creating some new ones, see the "Meow Generator" at https://motherboard.vice.com/en_us/article/a3dn9j/this-deep-learning-ai-generated-thousands-of-creepy-cat-pictures.
63 Susskind and Susskind, *The Future of the Professions: How Technology Will Transform the Work of Human Experts*.

by prediction and generation, is bolstered by the inputs and outputs of analysis and simulation; the resulting expenditure of enormous social capital — both material and treasure — can occur with greater surety. This changes the fundamental value of architecture itself in a social context by creating insights and protocols connected to the performative outcomes of buildings and a stronger provable correlation between the assertions of a design and the actual results created by the use and experience of the building itself.

Science, beauty, performance and use

A final note on the efficacy of computation as a threat to the aesthetic and technical autonomy of the architect. Schumacher suggests: "I am not turning architecture into a science. This cannot be done. Architecture is not true but useful/beautiful."[64] Perhaps this is accurate, although there are certainly important components of architecture that are more than useful and performative. It will be up to architects to decide the role of computation in the Second Machine Age, and particularly the extent to which they want to cede decisions and responsibility to machines. The Susskinds believe this is inevitable as some level. But all of us might best heed the words of Harvard social scientist David Yankelovich, who coined what is known as the McNamara Fallacy. Robert McNamara was John F. Kennedy's Secretary of Defense during the Vietnam War known for demanding purely quantitative data to make decisions. Yankelovich warns:

> The first step is to measure whatever can be easily measured. This is OK as far as it goes. The second step is to disregard that which can't be easily measured or to give it an arbitrary quantitative value. This is artificial and misleading. The third step is to presume that what can't be measured easily really isn't important. This is blindness. The fourth step is to say that what can't be easily measured really doesn't exist. This is suicide.[65]

---

64 Schumacher Vienna IOA Silver Lecture.
65 David Yankelovich, "Corporate Priorities: A Continuing Study of the New Demands on Business," in *Daniel Yankelovich Inc* (Stamford, CT: Daniel Yakelovich Inc., 1972). As cited in Wikipedia at https://en.wikipedia.org/wiki/McNamara_fallacy.

3

methodology

3.1

Procedures, Process and Outcomes

Do digital tools make design more potent? How do precision, iteration, analysis, measurement, optimization improve design?

Underlying the undertaking of this book is an inherent question: is technology merely another instrument in architecture, or is it a determining factor with important and unavoidable implications and, as a consequence, does it present a fundamental opportunity to change design methodology and as such the role of the architect? Answering this question demands a definition of design itself, which has been explored elsewhere (see Chapter 2.1, "The Digital Transformation of Design") in the distinction between the architect's responsibility to solve wicked and tame problems, and further to bridge the gaps between her intent — defined as the artifacts of her professional services — and first construction (execution) and ultimately building use (efficacy). The labor economist Paolo Tombesi sets forth a relatively straightforward definition of design that defers, at least for the moment, questions of the ineffable, aesthetic or cultural responsibilities of the architect: "(I)t is useful to take a prosaic view of design as a problem-defining, problem-solving, information-structuring activity that, on the basis of understood conditions and rules (however partial or 'rationally bounded'), defines a specific course of action."[1] Tombesi goes on to further position the acts of architectural design in terms of production:

> One is, of course, entitled to wonder what "producing architecture" exactly means, and whether it refers to the production of the building, the production of the ideas that go into defining the building, or the production of the information artifacts that are used to instruct and monitor the process of building. Indeed, architectural culture has always found it difficult reaching clarity on this, partly because of the objectively ambiguous nature of "services" in the production process,

---

1   Paolo Tombesi, "On the Cultural Separation of Design Labor," in Peggy Deamer and Phillip G. Bernstein (eds.), *Building (in) the Future: Recasting Labor in Architecture* (New York: Princeton Architectural Press, 2010), p. 119.

and partly because of the struggle, altogether peculiar to the discipline, in reconciling the intellectual nature of professional work with the economic aspects of the métier.[2]

Producing complex architecture

We will stipulate here that the potency of design — in order to 'produce architecture' — lies in creating and executing ideas in the service of both the technical and the aesthetic, and that even in the simplest terms, digital and computational technology has improved the architect's ability to produce, iterate and visualize design ideas. These are capabilities that, if skillfully deployed, improve the likelihood of achieving the ineffable. Of interest, however, is how the design process is made more potent by other dimensions of technological prowess; how tools that increase precision through prediction, make iteration more efficient, measure results, provide analytical insight and generally allow an architect to manage the complexity of architectural production change and improve design itself. To the extent that this proves true, any improvements in the means of architectural production, if carefully managed, will likely have the potential of improving what Tombesi calls the "intellectual nature of professional work."

The best demonstration of this relationship is found in Patrik Schumacher's definition of Parametricism (see Chapter 2.5, "Building Performance Design," for a more complete analysis), as "a new style rather than just... a new set of techniques. The techniques in question — the employment of animation, simulation and form-finding tools, as well as parametric modeling and scripting — have inspired a new collective movement with radically new ambitions and values."[3] His practice, Zaha Hadid Architects, 'finds forms' by using technological tools to model and integrate parametric characteristics of a project, and Schumacher has declared the need for "Parametricism 2.0" as "architecture's answer to contemporary, computationally empowered civilization,... the only architectural style that can take full advantage of the computational revolution that now drives all domains of society."[4] In this understanding of parametric design, computation provides the digital data inputs, computational protocols (scripts) and form-generating tools that result not just in provocative architectural form, but in a quest for an entirely new architectural style that may be more impactful, ultimately, than Modernism itself.

The computational versus the digital

Let us leave the larger aesthetic and cultural questions to those more able to argue them for now, and turn to Schumacher's list of enabling technologies, which comprise instruments with specific implications for the nature of design work writ large. There are two horizons of implications for the computa-

2   Ibid.
3   Patrik Schumacher, "Parametricism Manifesto" (2008).
4   Patrik Schumacher and ebrary Inc., "Parametricism 2.0: Rethinking Architecture's Agenda for the 21st Century," http://site.ebrary.com/lib/yale/Doc?id=11251744, p. 10.

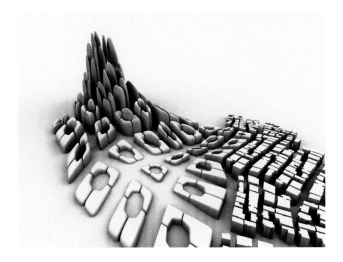

tional age in architecture. To examine them we draw on Stan Allen's distinction between the computational and the digital:

> At Princeton we've been trained very well... to refer not to the digital but to computation when we're talking about the computer in architectural terms... The digital is a kind of state of being. It's a condition. When you talk about computation, you're talking about active processes.[5]

Architectural production has been largely digital since the move to desktop computers and computer-aided drafting combined with word processing, spreadsheets and email replacing their analog counterparts. Along with this change came increased precision and accessibility; the geometric data that comprised computerized graphical drawings was far more accurate than its analog counterparts, since every line drawn in AutoCAD was represented at fullscale and to $1/10,000^{th}$ of a unit precision. Accompanying text was spell-checked, perfectly formatted and repeatable, and hand-tabulated columns of numbers gave way to the exactitudes of Excel. At this stage, digital renderings were essentially the compilation of high-resolution constructions in three dimensions, perfectly texture-mapped and with every shadow in place, but inaccessible artifacts, 3D snapshots of a design in a static state that were comprised of only imagery. All of the resulting digital data could be cop-

---

5   Stan Allen, "The Paperless Studios in Context," in *When Is the Digital in Architecture?*, p. 386.

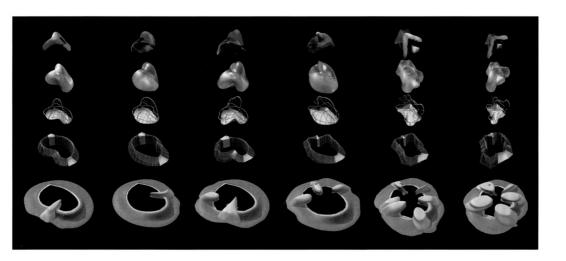

ied, almost instantly moved to collaborators, and stored for future reference. The digital, in this emphatic sense, was a necessary first step to the opportunities of the computational.

"Blobmeisters"

The early proponents of Parametricism, the "Blobmeisters" as Yale's former dean Robert Stern often called them, were leveraging the first computational capabilities of the digital, to wit, the use of the computer to generate the forms that result from complex mathematical calculations like NURBS (non-uniform rational basis splines), with algorithms making these forms possible, accessible and manipulable. The computer both managed the computation needed to depict these curves, i.e., all the data required to represent them, and generated the outputs to computer-controlled fabrication devices that built them. Early computation thus provided the first 'digital through line' from intent to execution, leveraging what computers do best: crunch very accurate numbers, allow the generation of lots of options (which, in their digital as opposed to physical form, can be created effortlessly and without the cost of their hand-crafted predecessors like drawings and scale models), and provide the resulting performance measurements of the results.

Computing performance

Since Greg Lynn's original work in the late 1980s the extensive use of computation seems to have been associated almost exclusively with the proclivity to generate blobs, or at least large-scale, fluid, extensive smooth surfaces as a primary architectural move. This was an understandable direction, as blobs and curves leverage some of computation's most accessible opportunities: surface generation, as well as structural and material behaviors. The shape,

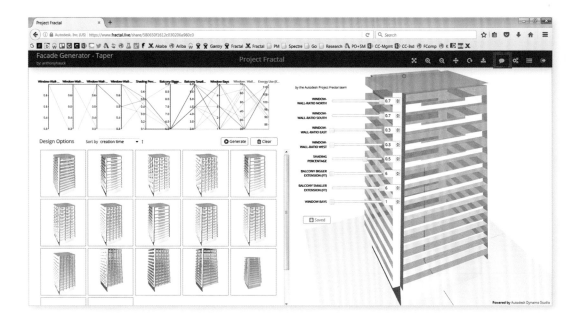

stability and porosity of a material are well understood and can be modeled parametrically and manipulated computationally with relative ease, and even optimized. As Philippe Block declared in Schumacher's recent compilation of all things Parametric, "(t)he terms 'expressive' and 'structurally efficient' are no longer oxymoronic, but can be synonymous."[6] Figure 3.1.1 shows 3.1.1 an urban planning proposal by Zaha Hadid Architects based on social, economic and physical parameters as a generator of form while Figure 3.1.2 is an 3.1.2 early example by Greg Lynn of his so-called "Embryological House" design.

Today we are entering an age of new computational capabilities and with it, new architectural possibilities. The tools that drove our fascination with form and structure were largely geometric in nature — think Rhino (and its scripting engine Rhinoceros), CATIA and even AutoCAD, tied in some cases to structural analysis engines and dependent almost entirely on representational strategies: how various scripted inputs generated or morphed forms and shapes directly. Representation strategies have expanded dramatically, however, in the era of building information modeling. Geometry is but one aspect of BIM, and (at least in theory) a much wider array of design parameters have become available for computational manipulation. And as all tools

6   Philippe Block, "Parametricism's Structural Congeniality," *Architectural Design* 86, no. 02 (2016), "Parametricism 2.0: Rethinking Architecture's Agenda for the 21st Century," ed. Patrik Schumacher, p. 70.

3.1.4 Performance parameters of a curtain wall

Performance Characteristics	Parameters
Facade expression	Geometry, dimensions, material choice
Structural performance	Unit performance, connection, system behavior
Weather barrier, rain screen	Connections, gaskets
Energy barrier	U-Value, thermal transmittance
Acoustic barrier	Sound transmission co-efficient
Daylight controller	Glass transmissivity, transparency, shading performance
System cost	Materials, labor, market conditions, installation sequence
Embodied carbon	Material characteristics, delivery approach, manufacturing approach
Construction sequence	Installation strategy

3.1.3 are further turbo-charged by a move from the desktop to the cloud, BIM-based representation (and other computational technologies) will be free of the constraints that have challenged the ability to represent very large, parametrically complex projects. Figure 3.1.3 shows a script driving BIM parameters to generate a solution.

Let us take the simple example of a curtain wall system enclosing a building. That particular element plays several different roles in the design: expressive facade, structural element, weather protector, energy conservator, acoustic barrier, daylight controller. Decisions about the curtain wall system have major implications for the construction strategy, cost and building performance of a project. Only a limited number of the implications of the curtain wall design, as controlled by the architect, can be represented by geometry manipulated by scripts; an integrated view of the design as it relates to the totality of the systems of construction, performance and delivery is required. Figure 3.1.4 shows a tabulation of such characteristics.

3.1.4 While it might be possible to understand, define and optimize each of these characteristics in isolation, their effects on the building occur in concert. A change in the dimensions of the mullion system, for example, changes the weight, amount of glass and insulation value of the entire system itself, and has direct implications on the building structure (how does the frame carry the wall, and how is it connected?) and the building mechanical systems (how do changes in the heating/cooling load affect air distribution, sizing of air conditioning, etc.?). The representation of the system as more than geometry (in other words, representation in BIM) connected to analytical engines (like shadow projection, heating/cooling load calculators, structural performance, acoustic performance) gives the modern designer the inputs necessary to make an optimized decision and gain a clear view to what variables in the design equation can be manipulated in order to achieve specific goals.

Computing alternatives

Computation within the individual applications that create our curtain wall representation and its resulting analytical outputs are the first horizon of opportunity. The second is using algorithms to set the performance objectives of the overall system — the objective outputs resulting from design decisions and adjustments — and then allowing those self-same algorithms to generate a broad set of options for the designer to consider. Our architect designing this curtain wall may be looking at trade-offs between the ratio of solid to void and available daylight in the spaces next to the wall itself. Making this determination is a design choice, not an optimization problem. Robust representation platforms like BIM, combined with analytical engines that report on the results of decisions, rationalize but do not replace the designer's judgment; the range of options is greatly enlarged and more easily understood. Ultimately, however, final conclusions are a result of the designer's judgment about trade-offs and opportunities, and not the manifest destiny of a computer's code. Mark Burry's contribution to Parametricism in a recent issue of *AD* makes this admonition: "Personally, I favour and deliberate design process that keeps digital agency firmly under the control of the architect and at some distance ahead of any careless deployment of someone else's algorithm, or the embrace of the accident and other related happenstances."[7]

An algorithm is not blissfully rational and free from the inherent leanings of its designer. There is legitimate concern that systems that encode the implicit biases of their designers, or datasets that are a result of biased outcomes, can skew the output of computational decision-making support. Recent research has discovered these problems in algorithms used to compute prison sentences, programs originally lauded for their decidedly "non-human" decision-making.[8]

Precision, ambiguity, complexity

The definition of precision expands in this context to an understanding of interconnected resolution of a design decision, and by extension to further control over the implications of the design. If pre-digital design was an exercise in speculative prediction almost entirely reliant on experience, intuition and judgment, computational design moves to analytical prediction bolstered by the assurance that a wider set of alternatives has been explored and evaluated. By expanding the range of exploration, analytical prediction

7 Mark Burry, "Essential Precursors to the Parametricism Manifesto: Antoni Gaudi and Frei Otto," *Architectural Design* 86, p. 34.
8 Will Knight, "Biased Algorithms Are Everywhere, and No One Seems to Care," *MIT Technology Review* (2017), https://www.technologyreview.com/s/608248/biased-algorithms-are-everywhere-and-no-one-seems-to-care/.

3.1.5 Comparison images of 'File Explorer' versus Web-based file organization

emboldens the designer and gives her, by extension, more control over the final product. Intuition and judgment are strategies to manage ambiguity and reduce complexity, and the methodologies recommended here reduce ambiguity and simultaneously manage the increased complexity of building itself. If early parametricists supported form-making with specific analytical tools (like structural optimizers), their successor designers will interconnect the results of several different such engines to generate an entirely new, and unanticipated, set of results. Even Schumacher is beginning to tout such possibilities, arguing that 'Parametricism 2.0' incorporates the insights and design parameters from crowd simulations, social interaction and urban design characteristics. As a bottom line, the analytical foundations surely expand the solution space through predictive insight even further.[9]

Representational platforms like cloud-enabled BIM will connect various analytical engines designed to evaluate and optimize the 'unambiguous' characteristics of a design. Structural performance, air temperature and flow, even crowd behavior can be directly modeled by hard-coded algorithms, and their results 'cross-connected' by adjusting the performance of parameters in a BIM representation. Emergent generations of evaluative tools will make even these tools seem limited, as machine learning techniques allow computers to reason inferentially about design by looking at large pools of design and performance data.

Performance-driven design

Consider the following scenario: a firm specializing in health care design has accumulated hundreds of BIM datasets from projects executed over the past ten years. At the same time, their clients have collected performance information from sensors incorporated into digital building control systems that record systems behaviors, ambient temperatures, energy consumption and other resource use. That same client's business management system has exacting records of staff time spent, correlated with security sensor systems that record staff locations and movements. Today's machine learning platforms can look across these enormous digital 'lakes' of data and draw conclusions about the correlations between design decisions (represented in the BIM data) and resulting building and staff performance, recommending best practices evidenced by the relationships. This is an example of a self-reinforcing predictive analytic system which grows stronger as more and more data becomes available. Early experiments in machine learning for building performance are underway: at the time of this writing, research teams at Autodesk have built a machine learning system to 'study' construction management information from collections of large projects and predict where risks of failure in subcontractor performance are likely to occur. Such insight is just the beginning of the next generation of analytics, and is an early indication that the 'economic performance' of projects, as anticipated by Tombesi, will soon be assimilated into the computational analytical infrastructure that will drive design.

New means of collaboration and coordination

More robust representational and analytic tools are not the complete story of technology's likely impact on the procedures and processes of design. Computational process both enables new complexity in the design itself and de-

---

9 Schumacher and ebrary Inc., "Parametricism 2.0: Rethinking Architecture's Agenda for the 21st Century."

3.1.6 Modern collaboration (Large Model Viewer)

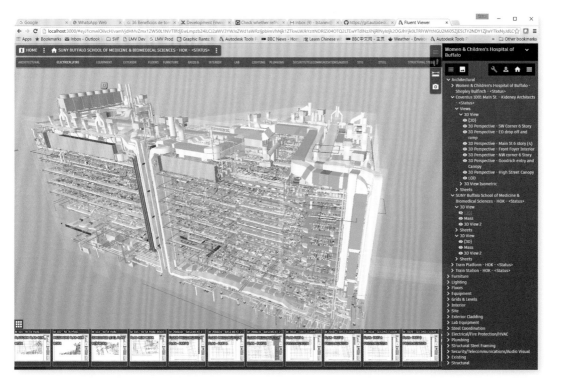

3.1.7 Colocation room

3.1.5   mands a simultaneous improvement in the infrastructure of collaboration.[10]
Producing architecture means sufficient control over the means of production, including the various collaborators and contributors to that process,
particularly the constellation of engineering and technical consultants nec-

10 In this case, "infrastructure" refers to the computational systems used to connect project teams together and manage
both their data and their workflows. Early such systems, primarily web-based, only provided a secure place to park
data so it could be shared. More sophisticated systems emerging today manage version control, flow of information
between players, and both synchronous (think chat or texting) and asynchronous (email) communication.

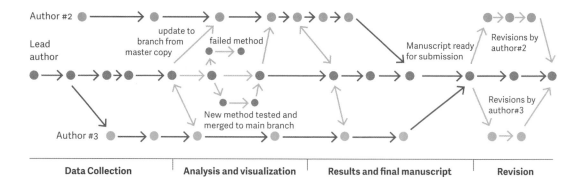

Author #2

Lead author

Author #3

update to branch from master copy

failed method

New method tested and merged to main branch

Manuscript ready for submission

Revisions by author#2

Revisions by author#3

Data Collection	Analysis and visualization	Results and final manuscript	Revision

essary to accomplish a modern project. And like the tools of representation and analysis, collaboration technologies are moving away from replicating the transactions of the analog age. With the advent of the internet came an array of 'collaboration platforms' (like Sharepoint, or today's Google Docs) that essentially organize, manage and monitor the exchange of digital information, making same more accessible and its use auditable for risk purposes. Building teams working today have more integrative tools that allow them to share models interactively, view them dynamically and assemble necessary data rapidly via cloud technology. And with modern video technology, even physical location is no longer determinative. The challenge, of course, arrives when each of these teams is creating, evaluating and integrating enormous ranges of options and detailed design decisions into the overall complex of the design enterprise.

    In particular, the methodologies of modern software development are beginning to affect traditional means of building production collaboration. Just as car manufacturer Toyota's Lean methodology is changing construction, 'agile development,' a method of working together on complex, ambiguous projects, may show the way for design. The creation of complex software is dependent on larger teams of engineers to create it, and agile is one technique of several invented by the software industry to allow those teams to work together. The days of creating a very detailed, comprehensive design and a similarly specific plan to build the code base have given way to an approach where a team agrees on the higher-order characteristics of a design and then works in rapid iterations toward the intermediate goal. Each iteration is called a 'sprint,' during which sub-teams work on their component contributions and at the end of which the pieces are merged and coordinated. The process is supported by a dual approach called CI/CD or 'continuous integration/continuous delivery,' where automated content management systems (the most well-known of which is called GITHUB, see

Collaboration platforms

3.1.6, 3.1.7

Agile development, a method of working together on complex, ambiguous projects

Figure 3.1.8) combined with automated testing routines allow small pieces of work to be constantly tested and integrated into the overall work product. Given increasingly complex data structures and procedures, it is likely that architectural production will adapt some version of such processes, giving architects an opportunity to leverage all the possibilities of computational design while simultaneously creating an obligation to understand and control the protocols that create progress.

Determinate context

An intangible form in an indeterminate context

The architect and mathematician Christopher Alexander once suggested that architectural design was the obligation to create " an intangible form in an indeterminate context,"[11] perhaps an apt description of Peter Rowe's 'wicked problem' characterization of the design process. Framing, constraining, iterating, selecting, and integrating design explorations into a synthetic solution means somehow managing the myriad considerations that an architect faces when designing a building, and controlling the sheer number of variables involved is an indeterminate process that relies as much on the rational analysis of the problem as the designer's intuition about how to solve it. But computation makes the indeterminate far less so, in that it provides rational inputs to a variety of problems that frame the required outcomes of the design itself. As the analysis of such inputs becomes routinely available to architects, their proposed solutions can be presented on clear, demonstrable set of analytical conclusions. This is an opportunity to enhance the capabilities and credibility of architects and their design prowess.

The ineffable aspects of architectural production will always also be intangible by definition, as will the cultural, aesthetic and social contexts from which they spring. The best architecture will derive from both rational and ineffable decisions. As aspects of the production of the built artifact itself, and the architect's role in producing it, become increasingly evidentiary and provable, and generated by intelligent, computational processes there is an inherent danger. That which can be routinized can also be commodified, and the ease with which computation — in the form of advanced modeling, AI and algorithims — may automate the making of buildings means robot architects could squeeze out the ineffable as a result. It will be incumbent upon architects to demonstrate that real design is better than the banal conclusions of the machines.

11 Christopher Alexander, *Notes on the Synthesis of Form* (Cambridge, MA: Harvard University Press, 1964), p. 26.

3.2

Information Coherence

Is the creation and control of information systems by architects necessary for the design and construction of buildings?

Any design process can be characterized as a systematic exploration of alternatives at successive levels of refinement and precision, leading to supportable conclusions. In the case of architecture, the inherent decisions are bolstered by graphic and textual documentation acting as both guideposts and detailed instantiations of selected alternatives and resulting conclusions. The resulting information, often characterized as the architect's 'instruments of service,' are not only the products of the architect's efforts but rather constitute the vectors by which decision-making is made real. The same is true as successive levels of contribution to the building design enterprise (by, for example, engineers and other consultants) are layered into the evolving decision-making process, creating a vast, interconnected network of information. But the architect alone has the responsibility for directing the flow of this information, coordinating its production and distribution, and assuring its integration into a coherent whole as the design is developed.

The logic of two dimensions

The architects of the Egyptian pyramids scribed site plans on stone tablets, just as their modern counterparts shape a building design in three-dimensional virtual data space. In the pre-digital age, design information was rendered permanent and referrable by committing it to paper. Drawings of various scales depicted the design (plans, sections, details); text described its performative characteristics (engineering calculations, specifications); narratives documented progress and decisions (meeting minutes, correspondence, transmittals); other myriad sheets filled project files to memorialize information referenced by the project team. Over the course of a project, storage cabinets — flat files and racks for drawing sets, file drawers for the rest of the stuff — filled with related paper that was the representation of both the design and the process the design team used to define it.

Those paper records lent a certain logic and discipline to information management before computers, and well-organized projects followed pre-

SECTION F — PROJECT RECORDS: FILING AND STORAGE
OFFICE MANUAL
JANUARY 2015

3.00 REVIEW AGENCIES

3.01 Code and Zoning Requirements/Analysis
3.02 Permits & Fees / Permit Log / Bonds (Agency)
3.03 Application Forms (Blank)
3.04 Planning Department Correspondence
3.05 Conditions of Approval/Findings/Reports
3.06 Building Department Correspondence
3.07 Plan Check Corrections
3.08 Fire Department Correspondence
3.09 Public Works/Engineering Department Correspondence
3.10 Grading Department Correspondence
3.11 OSHA Correspondence
3.12 Homeowners Association
3.13 Other Review Agency Correspondence
3.14 Electric Company Correspondence
3.15 Water Company Correspondence
3.16 Gas Campany Correspondence
3.17 Telephone Company Correspondence
3.18 Cable Co. Correspondence
3.19 Other Utility Company Correspondence
3.20 Green Building Certification Institute (GBCI)
3.21 LEED Letter Templates
3.22 LEED Credit Interpretation Request (CIR)

Files may be added for additional agency and
utility company correspondence.

4.00 CONSULTANTS

4.01 Architect — Correspondence
4.02 Structural — Correspondence
4.03 HVAC — Correspondence
4.04 Plumbing — Correspondence
4.04 HVAC/Plumbing — Correspondence
4.05 Fire Protection — Correspondence
4.06 Title 24 — Correspondence
4.07 Electrical — Correspondence
4.08 Civil Engineering — Correspondence
4.09 Soils — Correspondence
4.10 Site/Building Assessment — Correspondence
4.11 Seismic Assessment — Correspondence
4.12 Excavation/Shoring — Correspondence
4.13 Environmental Impact Report (EIR) — Correspondence
4.14 Traffic — Correspondence
4.15 Graphics/Signage — Correspondence
4.16 Parking — Correspondence
4.17 Landscaping — Correspondence
4.18 Specifications — Correspondence

SECTION F — PROJECT RECORDS: FILING AND STORAGE
OFFICE MANUAL
JANUARY 2015

4.00 CONSULTANTS (CONT.)

4.19 Interior Design — Correspondence
4.20 Acoustical — Correspondence
4.21 Lighting — Correspondence
4.22 Food Service — Correspondence
4.23 Illustrator — Correspondence
4.24 Model Maker — Correspondence
4.25 Architectural Photo — Correspondence
4.26 Estimating — Correspondence
4.27 Leasing — Correspondence
4.28 Special Inspections/Testing — Correspondence
4.29 CAD — Correspondence
4.30 Property Inspections — Correspondence
4.31 Communications — Correspondence
3.32 Sound and Video — Correspondence
4.33 Commissioning
4.34 LEEP AP — Correspondence (file LEED letter templates
      in REVIEW AGENCIES folder 3.19)

Files may be added for additional consultant
correspondence.

5.00 SURVEYS, TESTS AND REPORTS

5.01 Soils
5.02 Survey
5.03 Structural Calculations
5.04 Title 24
5.05 Environmental
5.06 Legal/Title Report
5.07 Site/Building Assessment
5.08 Seismic Assessment
5.09 Property CC & R'S
5.10 Special Inspections/Testing
5.11 Real Estate Marketing Reports/Analysis
5.12 Property Inspections
5.13 Storm Drainage

Do not include correspondence. Cover letters should be
filled under the appropriate agency and consultant, and a
copy may be attached to the report for reference.

6.00 MATERIALS RESEARCH AND SPECIFICATIONS

6.01 General Requirements
6.02 Site Construction
6.03 Concrete
6.04 Masonry

---

scribed protocols for structuring it. Organizing schema made finding the pieces of paper easier but also added an important benefit — the ability to scrub the project record of irrelevant or potentially litigation-inducing information. A well-curated project record was not just a talisman of what happened but was carefully expunged of records that could be distracting or otherwise difficult should a project get in trouble in court. Standards for record retention, based on risk management strategies and statutes of repose, dictated what should remain — and what should be destroyed — in the project information set.

Repose, the time period during which an error in the design must be discovered to be the subject of a lawsuit

Curating the project record

Of course, architects were largely uninterested in such things and informational hygiene in the pre-digital era was haphazard at best. The completion of a project meant the beginning of a new one, not a time for carefully massaging the project files for posterity. Warehouses of boxed files (and, eventually, tapes, and diskettes), full of interesting surprises, were the result. Should those boxes need to be paged from storage, likely by someone uninvolved in the project, reassembling the project record coherently was challenging at best and impossible at worst, because beyond the paper artifacts, the process of executing that project was actually a result of the orchestration of information in several modalities, only some of which are reconstructible from physical evidence and others not, including:

— **Communicating** who was working with whom, when, and about what? What interactions occurred that moved the design forward and, as a consequence, who knew what information and when?

— **Iterating and Versioning** what alternatives were examined, and how were they vetted, explained, culled, and chosen? How were selected alternatives properly integrated into the evolving design? What distinguished a valid alternative from a bad idea? When, if ever, did an earlier alternative inform the development of a later idea?

— **Referencing** what supporting information informed the design, and/or was incorporated into the design by reference? Were standard details instantiated by reference, modified, or just examined?

— **Sequencing** in what order were ideas examined and elaborated? Were they developed systematically or haphazardly by the designers, and if the latter, how were they integrated into the flow of the design?

Each of these activities is implicit in the job of the architect as both the leader and the orchestrator of the design process, implying obligations that are more than just careful record-keeping. Structuring, coordinating, editing, curating — in short — controlling the overall nature and flow of project information — is at the center of the architect's responsibility in order to both find and implement the best ideas in the service of the project. So to assure the proper progress of the design work itself, the architect (or someone) must be responsible not just for the organization of project information, but for its coherence.

From paper to digital

These responsibilities become more complex and profound in the digital age. Of course, digital tools have actually increased the volume of physical outputs as these are much easier to produce. But the digital format of the record itself creates new challenges, obligations and opportunities for the architect's control of the design process.

Consider the array of digital artifacts that populate the current software-empowered design process. First, models in multiple forms and generated from multiple sources are keystones of the evolving design representation. Those models, which may originate as pure geometry (from, say, Rhino) or more robust behaviorally descriptive building information models (BIM, e.g. from Revit or ArchiCAD), are likely supported by additional analytical models, either directly correlated to the geometry (from a structural analysis package like Tekla) or non-geometrically based simulations (such as cost estimates). Each of these model representations exists in various states of resolution, depending on the evolution of the design, and in multiple iterations

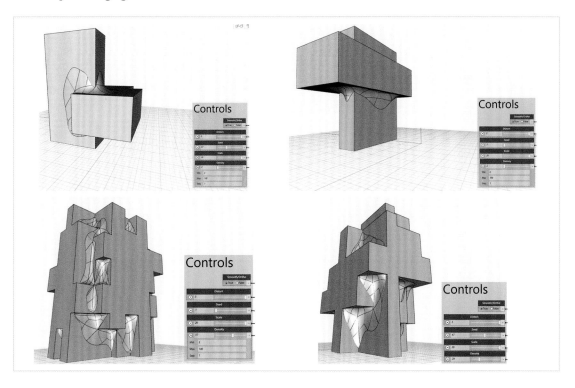

as alternatives are developed. Some aspects of the design will likely continue to be described in traditional orthographics like plan, section or elevation, even if these data are depicted as digital CAD files. Discipline-specific models (like BIM) contain extensive non-geometric metadata that imbues the representation with physical, performative or other descriptive characteristics. And at the time of writing in 2018, the use of computational design is increasing dramatically as scripting tools combined with modeling tools create another class of design information. While geometry representing a design solution was once directly manipulated by the designer using software, design solutions today can be partially generated by scripts, computerized recipes that iterate and generate solutions for the designer's consideration. This strategy is discussed in several other places in this book (see, for example, Chapters 2.3, "The Evolution of Responsible Control and Professional Care", and 4.3, "Calibrating Design Values"), but for the purposes of this chapter's examination scripts are yet another part of the project record and the information approach for design. The model shown in Figure 3.2.2 has thousands of instantiations. How are they part of the project record?

One element, multiple relationships

A simple example illuminates the complexity of the representational and information organization challenge. A door embedded deep in the interior ar-

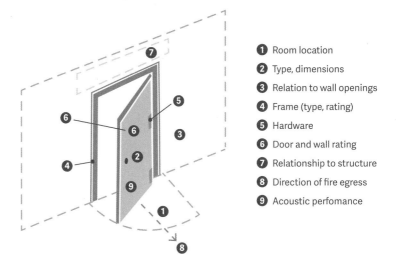

1. Room location
2. Type, dimensions
3. Relation to wall openings
4. Frame (type, rating)
5. Hardware
6. Door and wall rating
7. Relationship to structure
8. Direction of fire egress
9. Acoustic perfomance

chitecture of the building has an absolute location in space, defined dimensions (length, width and height) as well as additional descriptive data including its finish and color, direction of swing, hardware requirements, fire rating and related door frame. Somewhere the cost of purchasing and installing this door exists in a cost model. The door and frame together may be connected to an associated structural member (like a door lintel or nearby beam), giving the door a relationship to the structural behavior of the building (and the structural analytical model). The door may be in the direction of travel for fire exiting, meaning it also participates in the life safety system of the building. It may separate two acoustically isolated rooms, meaning it must be soundproofed along with its frame, which will require special appropriate installation. If a window is required in the door, suddenly the door becomes a complex object comprised of both a door element and a window and the window itself adds another level of detail. Early in its life as a design solution the door is likely generically described as a simple element without elaboration, but in order for that door to be made real it must be imbued, in some way, with all this geometric data and metadata, some of which might reside in the BIM, some in other models needed for fabrication, other metadata in specifications, cut sheets, fabrication orders, delivery manifests and so on. Only then can it be identified, ordered, fabricated, shipped, stored and

3.2.3   eventually installed properly by the builder.

The data comprising the door explained above is almost entirely first the responsibility of the architect, and then the door manufacturer and then the builder; it is thus isolated from the rest of the design team (engineers and other consultants) and as such is pretty straightforward. But building

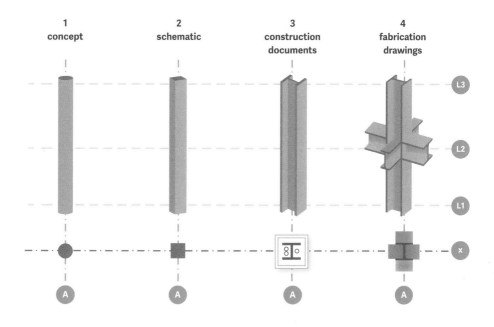

design in the digital age is a constellation of multivalent digital models and representations across various disciplines which must be coordinated and, as described above, coherent. Critical elements of buildings live, representationally, in the province of multiple designers and builders, who share responsibility for defining and integrating that element into the whole.

A column that supports the building near the door described above is such an element. From the architect's perspective, that column is part of the continuous structural frame stretching from the foundation to the underside of the roof. The structural engineer, however, knows that it acts as a singular unit that does its job between the frames of the floor and ceiling on the floor on which it resides and must be designed and detailed accordingly. The architect may clad the column in finishes that match the rest of the room in which it stands; the space between that finish and the structure itself is an opportunity for the electrical engineer to run conduit, the mechanical engineer to place a roof drain, and the fire protection engineer to embed smoke detectors. The designers of each of these systems that converge around the column describe their intent and result from the point of view of their individual design strategies, techniques and tools. The fabricators of each element have their own specific concerns about sizes, connections and the order of installation and use their specific approaches to resolve them. In current practice it falls to the architect to assure the parts work together as a whole, and to the builder to assure they are assembled logically, correctly and efficiently. Getting to this design/construction nirvana means

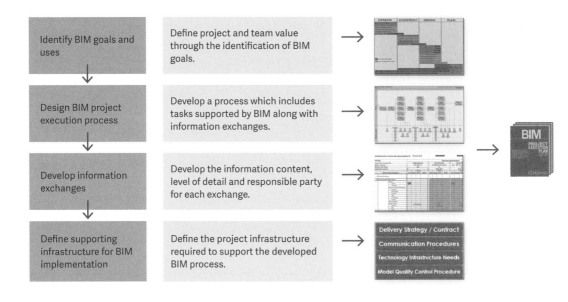

3.2.4 the multiplicity of digital representations produced by everyone must play well together, as suggested in Figure 3.2.4.

The emerging information complex

Thus the information complex (of a digitally enabled design and construction project) is comprised of multiple, discontinuous and heterogeneous representations of geometry, systems, annotations and procedures spanning across the sub-disciplines of design (architecture, engineering, other consulting) and construction (construction management, fabrication, supply chain management, installation). The challenge to manage it is not unlike many that architects faced in the past when construction itself became more problematic — with the most illuminating shifts appearing during the liability crisis of the 1980. At that time, designing buildings became much riskier as the complexity of the building enterprise increased. Fast-tracked projects demanded construction managers who would coordinate the sequence of construction in detail. Abating asbestos and brown-field sites led to the emergence of specialty consultants willing to take the attendant risks of remediation. Accelerated schedules and high interest rates made cost estimation complicated and risky, and contractors and other consultants emerged to fill a gap that architects, like in these other circumstances, were not willing to fill. Various theories exist as to why the remit of the architect deteriorated, particularly during this crisis. Insurance carriers proscribed services that they would allow architects to provide under their liability insurance coverage, and there were few objections by the profession at large

The liability crisis of the 1980s

to directions such as "don't design condominiums" or "don't be involved in asbestos." This aversion to risk was likely bolstered by tight fees paid by clients, making it less likely that designers wanted to assume any further risk of a lawsuit for which there would be no funds to defend. Finally, efforts in the United States by the AIA and other professional societies to exempt design professionals from any responsibility for construction means and methods so as to avoid any possible liability for construction worker safety convinced many clients and builders that architects were not interested in construction issues. In general, architects decided that these various responsibilities were unrelated to their core obligations as designers, without realizing that the resulting loss of influence and control compromised their actual influence over important design decisions and thus the efficacy of the profession itself. Disengagement from responsibility for cost and schedule — two of the central concerns of clients — were the most damaging losses in this regard.

The loss of the architects' influence

Managing the modern information complex is a similar opportunity for, or threat to, architects. What seemed, in the pre-digital late twentieth century, to be a tedious obligation to maintain good files and records now looks to be as important as the need to keep a project on the client's budget and schedule, because the proper control of information and its flow is now central to the project's success. In fact, one might argue that information control is a necessary condition for achieving budget, schedule and the architect's design objectives at the same time, replacing the pre-digital responsibility to coordinate the design through drawings.

BIM Execution Plan (BEP)

This concept is best understood in the emergence of the BIM Execution Plan (BEP) that is common to model-based projects today. The BEP is a planning tool used by digitally advanced project teams to plan their use of information. Much as Napoleon once suggested that "an army marches on its stomach," today's AEC teams march on coherent information and the BEP is the first and best chance to pre-ordain that logic. As described in Penn State's seminal *BIM Project Execution Planning Guide*:

> *A well-documented BIM Project Execution Plan will ensure that all parties are clearly aware of the opportunities and responsibilities associated with the incorporation of BIM into the project workflow. A completed BIM Project Execution Plan should define the appropriate uses for BIM on a project (e.g., design authoring, cost estimating, and design coordination), along with a detailed design and documentation of the process for executing BIM throughout a project's lifecycle.*[12]

3.2.5, 3.2.6

12 Computer Integrated Construction Research Program at the Pennsylvania State University, *Building Information Modeling Execution Planning Guide* (State College, PA: The Pennsylvania State University, 2010), p. i.

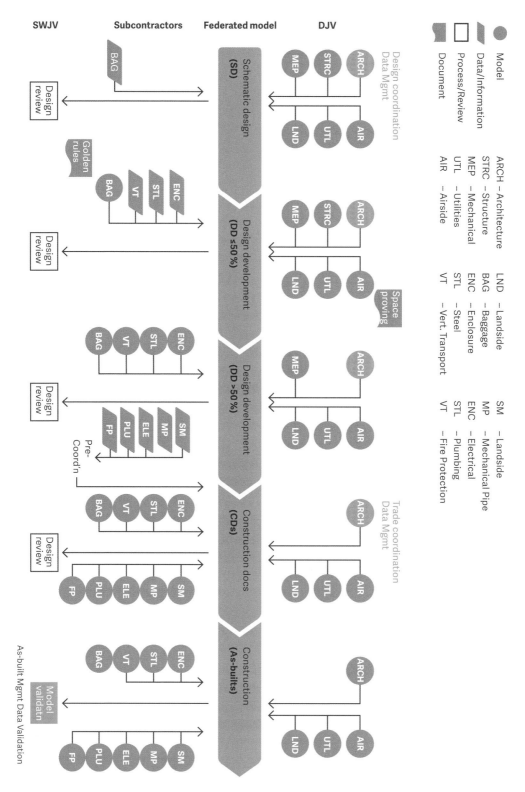

3.2.6 Model coordination timeline for an airport project

Legend:
- Model
- Data/Information
- Process/Review
- Document

ARCH – Architecture
STRC – Structure
MEP – Mechanical
UTL – Utilities
AIR – Airside

LND – Landside
BAG – Baggage
ENC – Enclosure
STL – Steel
VT – Vert. Transport

SM – Landside
MP – Mechanical Pipe
ENC – Electrical
STL – Plumbing
VT – Fire Protection

Columns: SWJV | Subcontractors | Federated model | DJV

Phases (Federated model):
- Schematic design (SD)
- Design development (DD ≤50%)
- Design development (DD >50%)
- Construction docs (CDs)
- Construction (As-builts)

Design coordination Data Mgmt

Trade coordination Data Mgmt

Space proving

SWJV elements: Design review, Golden rules, Pre-Coord'n, Model validat'n, As-built Mgmt Data Validation

Information design

Like many other strategic digital questions for the architect, the information approach for a project — that will dictate how the design unfolds and is implemented — is a design problem in and of itself that deserves the same care and attention as the project schedule and management plan. The architect's vision for the project is dependent upon this structure, and not in opposition to it, in that the flow and organization of information *is* the design, and, increasingly, the execution of the design in the field. Architects leave this job to professional data organizers, IT professionals, or other members of the design team at their peril.

Early indications in the era of BIM of the architect's engagement in this question are not promising. Firms recruit and cultivate 'BIM managers,' a role they see as distinct from, say, that of 'job captain.' The former is a data wrangler; the latter the person responsible for the technical coordination and integration of the project deliverables. There may be a generational challenge here: as the baby boomers (like me) leave the profession the technology anxiety of the elderly should fade as more digitally native architects lead firms. It may be that rapidly evolving tools and approaches for data control move too quickly for firms working on the slow rhythms of building projects to manage.

BIM managers versus job captains

Yet it has been my experience, in my days as a technology vendor, that architects largely consider problems of data organization, management and coordination to be either 'not architecture' (since it is not seen as central to design) or something to be delegated to a junior technologist or a software platform. But as I often advised our engineers when I was in the technology business, "software does not, and should not, substitute for project management." Choosing to lose control of design data should not be the next delegation of responsibility in the long train of loss of control by architects that began in the 1980s.

Coherence and control

To delegate the responsibility for information control leaves the profession vulnerable on other fronts as well, particularly as more modern approaches for information access and use evolve. Embedded in the big data that is the thousands of digital files of various formats that comprise today's AEC projects is a wealth of insight awaiting the proper search engine to mine it. As so aptly demonstrated by the logic imposed by Google on the information cacophony that is the internet, similar indexing tools will soon emerge for architects and builders, first allowing data to be discovered independent of project context in those files. A builder could look across projects to see how many steel frame jobs he might be bidding at a given time, and whether economies of scale were possible. An architect could examine the dimensional characteristics of the last ten schools she designed to interpolate ideal characteristics for the next classroom. As this strategy of indexicality makes project data sets increasingly valuable, the ability to deploy insights accumulated from the data on subsequent projects will become first a competitive advantage, and then a necessity. Organizing and controlling the origination of this data is the first step in gaining this advantage in value generation.

Beyond lies the untapped potential of tomorrow's internet of big data — machine learning, or artificial intelligence--now becoming both technically and commercially available. Just as Google has recently dramatically improved its 'Translate' services by using neural networks and algorithms that allow computers to 'learn' from enormous data sets,[13] one can imagine similar approaches that look across vast project data sets, including statistics about performance and project outcomes, to draw broad conclusions and recommend appropriate design strategies. This might sound like as if it portends the eventual replacement of designers by algorithms. For the untalented designers who produce prosaic results, perhaps so. But designing the best buildings will always require the intuition, insights and judgments of good, human designers supported by the best tools and working toward optimal outcomes. Project information can be a potent weapon in that arsenal — but only if architects decide to control it to their own ends and design the systems and strategies to leverage it.

13 Gideon Lewis-Kraus, "The Great A.I. Awakening," *The New York Times Magazine* (14 December 2016), https://www.nytimes.com/2016/12/14/magazine/the-great-ai-awakening.html.

3.3

Designing Design: Optimizing, Solving, Selecting

How do digital strategies for problem definition, generation, evaluation and optimization affect the architect's process and goals?

Irrespective of the use of particular tools or technologies, the design process at the heart of architectural production is generally comprised of discrete steps: setting of objectives, generation of alternatives, selection of an option, and refinement. Creating and optimizing concepts that evolve from strategic and conceptual through to specific and tectonic levels, and integrating those ideas into a holistic vision and plan for a building is the core of the architect's value to clients, the systems of delivery and society writ large.

Optimizing design choices

Implied in the design proposition is the question of optimization: how do you know that the option being explored, evaluated or selected is the best? The architect may apply a range of criteria toward that goal, from "in my judgment as an experienced designer, this is the right answer" to "this particular issue can be evaluated quantitatively, and based on the numbers, this is the answer." Perhaps this is the design continuum from the ineffable to the technical, or even the 'wicked' versus the 'tame' but there is another dimension to consider: the complexity of the evaluation strategy itself. Architectural designs are more often than not multi-variant, dependent upon an intricate interplay of factors ranging from aesthetic through technical to economic. The architect choosing glass for an exterior facade is balancing questions of appearance, performance, availability, purchase cost, installation and maintenance (to name a few). It is the ability to synthesize a selection strategy from these various strands of influence, multiplied by the thousands of such decisions ranging from design intent to execution, that is at the heart of the architectural design process and of the architect's unique role in the building production process.

Design inspiration can come from anywhere, and there are many degrees of freedom for an architect to generate a design. But there are prototypical structures and understood paradigms that frame the typical archi-

Normative practice

tectural design process in normative practice. In the US, there is a well-

Phases of service

	Feasibility	Concept	Detailed Design	Production Design	Procure	Construction	Close-out	Occupancy
United States (AIA Standard)	Predesign (PD)	Schematic Design (SD)	Design Development (DD)	Construction Documents (CD)	Bid (PR)	Construction Administration (CA)	Commission (CO)	
United Kingdom (RIBA plan of work)	Strat Def (0) / Brief (1)	Concept (2)	Developed Design (3)	Technical Design (4)		Construction (5)	Handover (6)	In Use (7)
Germany (HAOI)	First Consultation (1)	Preliminary Design (2)	Construct Dwgs (3) / Building Warrant Dwgs (4)	Detailed Building Design (5)	Prep (6) / Tender (7)	Site Inspection (8)	Document (9)	
Japan (Japanese Institute of Architects)	Kikaku (Planning)	Kihon Sekkei (Schematic Design)		Jissei Sekkei (Detail Design)	(Reconcile)	Gemba (Construction)		

understood construct called "basic services" that attempts to define, in shorthand form, what an architect might do on a "typical" project. It is usually comprised of standard stages of design like schematics, design development, etc., and is as much a way of bounding the expected services within a limited fee as a way of structuring the work. For example, under a typical understanding of basic services, the architect in the US will hire a structural engineer and a building services engineer under her fixed fee. Any additional engineers required for the project mean an increase in a "typical" basic services fee.

Basic services

Let us presume that the object of that process is to create a building for a client with an articulated need. For such a project, the generation of alternatives, selection of options and refinement of the selected ideas follows a larger progression of decision-making: an ordering of ideas (concepts about, for example, the overall organization and configuration of the building) that is followed by the design and selection of increasingly more detailed characteristics (like choices of materials or systems) and eventually the construction execution. In professional practice, this hierarchy of decision-making serves to make the design process legible to clients, the decision sequence more explicit, and assures that previous commitments become the basis of subsequent project development. The work should progress, in theory, in a logical fashion.

Progressions of design

This progression is understood in the United States to be the sequential phases of schematic design, design development, construction documents and so forth; in the UK, the Plan of Work comprises seven stages from 'Strategic Definition' (Phase 0) through 'In Use' (Phase 7); in Germany, the Official Scale of Fees for Services by Architects and Engineers (HOAI) Phases 1–9 such as first consultation through preliminary design, detailed building design and administration and documentation;[14] and the Japanese MLIT "Order of Public Building Phases."[15] Every construction market has its own bespoke definitions, terminology and standards for the structure of design to construction (or operation) that are a function of local custom and project delivery norms. They share, however, a common succession of design and construction phase resolution, summarized as follows and compared in Figure 3.3.1:

3.3.1

— **Problem definition** when the characteristics, aspirations and assumptions upon which the project will be designed and evaluated are determined. This definition, sometimes called the program or the brief, outlines at minimum selection of site, overall construction budget and schedule, as well as spatial requirements and functional characteristics.

— **Concept design** during which the basic design strategy and general configuration of the project is determined in terms of design idea, site positioning, size as well as the general arrangement of spaces, and key functional characteristics are described. Overall approaches to subsystems like structural and building services are outlined and chosen. Cost estimating is likely parametric, based on general area or volume calculations — a 'top down' estimate.

— **Detailed design** when the preliminary technical definition of the building is created and coordinated, including selection of finishes, key details, equipment and key sub-systems. An important result of the detailed design stage is the production of a quantitative, take-off-based cost estimate that defines or projects specific quantities of materials and labor necessary to build — a shift to a 'bottom-up' estimate.

— **Production design** creates the detailed construction documents that serve as the instructions to the contractor to build the project as well as the submission to regulatory authorities for a permission to build.

---

14 See the bilingual German and English edition, *HOAI 2013-Textausgabe auf Deutsch und auf Englisch Honorarordnung für Architekten und Ingenieure — Official Scale of Fees for Services by Architects and Engineers*, 5th ed. (Springer Vieweg, 2013).

15 Royal Institute of British Architects (ed.), "Riba Plan of Work" (London: RIBA, 2013), https://www.ribaplanofwork.com/PlanOfWork.aspx, and Japan Ministry of Land, Infrastructure and Transportation, "Order of Public Building Phases," in *MLIT* (Tokyo: MLIT, 2018) translated for the author by Keith Krolak. The RIBA plan was revised in 2012 to reflect new digital workflows and deliverables.

3.3.2 Example of a typical project schedule

Project Phase	M.	2018	2019	2020	2021	2022
		J J A S O N D	J F M A M J J A S O N D	J F M A M J J A S O N D	J F M A M J J A S O N D	J F M A M J J A S O N D
Architect Selection	–					
Master Planning Phase	2					
Pre Design	3					
MP/PD Major Milestones and Presentations to Owner	–	50% ◆ ◆ 100%				
PD Cost Estimating	–	● Pre design cost estimate				
Schematic Design	3					
SD Major Milestones and Presentations to Owner	–	50% ◆ ◆ 100%				
SD Cost Estimating	–	50% ● ● 100% SD cost estimate				
Design Development	8					
DD Major Milestones and Presentations to Owner	–	50% ◆ ◆ 100%				
DD Cost Estimating	–	50% ● ● 100% DD cost estimate				
Construction Documents	9					
CD Cost Estimates	–	50% ● ● 85% CD cost estimate				
Procurement	–	◆ ◆				
Construction	30					

Library project / Preliminary project schedule

- ▨ Design task
- ▨ Cost Model / Reconcile
- ▨ Owner Review
- ▨ Construction task
- ● Cost estimate
- ☆ Public Review / Charrette
- ◆ Presentation / Deliverables
- ◆ Bid Point

— **Procurement/construction** when the builder and team are selected, contracts negotiated, and the building constructed.

— **Close-out** when the building is tested and handed over to the client for use.

A schedule for an American project using this structure might look something like Figure 3.3.2. Each stage concludes with the release of a set of progressively more detailed documents that memorialize decisions and the state of the design.

3.3.2

The staging sequence provides a good, general framework for the progression of design activity and decisions that lead to a building, and it has been held generally true since the era of manual drafting and even through to the mature use of CAD. Each stage is discrete and progresses sequentially in linear fashion, resulting in a schedule sometimes described as a 'waterfall'.

'Waterfall' planning

How are ideas defined and memorialized?

(Models, metadata, drawings)

REPRESENTATION

How are ideas simulated and evaluated?

Simulation, analysis, scripting, optimization

ANALYSIS

How are ideas translated from digital to physical form?

Construction planning, procuring, assembling

REALIZATION

3D printing
Robotics
CNC/CAM
Laser screening
Commissioning

COLLABORATION
How are ideas captured, managed and shared?

Reference data   Project record   External knowledge

Representation changing the architect's services

But as informational and computational technologies have evolved and permeated the design process, changing the means of representation, analysis, realization and collaboration for architects and the overall building production team, the strategies for making design choices and the structure of decision-making have evolved in response, in order to leverage the technical capabilities of new tools, but also to reflect new realities and expectations of construction delivery. Many of these changes have been described in previous chapters, but to briefly recap, as shown again in Figure 3.3.3.

3.3.3

— **Representation** moved beyond drawings, digital or otherwise, to robust BIM-based models rich with information and parameters. Those models, and their 3D geometric counterparts, can be manipulated directly or via scripts and external algorithms.
— **Analysis and simulation** support representation with robust evaluation engines that provide direct computational conclusions about aspects of building performance, from structural characteristics through lighting and heating loads, and eventually to occupant behavior. As increasingly

large datasets are generated from representational and analytical tools, machine learning algorithms will generate further evaluations and insights of projects as they emerge.

— **Realization tools** mediate the divide between the digital and the physical, capturing information about the physical world and making it accessible to the digital (like laser scanning and 3D photography) or transferring digital instructions as design data to computationallydriven fabrication and construction processes.

— **Collaboration platforms** organize, monitor, test and distribute heterogeneous design information and manage complex interactive workflows between the parties of architectural production.

The work of architects has become more precise, information-rich and quantitative as a result as tools in each of these categories become standard fare in their portfolio. Digital data can serve more design processes, and those processes have become either supported by or entirely replaced by computational methods. Two examples on either extreme of the architect's services sequence illuminate this change: area computation and quantity calculations and construction logic and fabrication.

Computing quantities

When drawing was entirely manual, determining the quantitative characteristics of a project required extensive intermediating calculations with other tools. Understanding the gross and net area, of the designed building involved hand measurement and computation. After the advent of CAD, these data were extracted by manual circumscription of spaces with geometric boundaries whose interior area could be computed, an improvement in precision. Quantity calculations, a 'next order' computation involving more variables, required both direct measurement and then additional work to derive a result. Measuring the linear length of a wall in a plan, for example, would need to be paired with an equation that would derive the associated surface area of wallboard or paint. Computing the volume of a space would require a similar multi-step process, cross-indexing area information from a plan with sectional dimensions. For each progressive step in the development of the design, from concept through construction, the required information became more detailed and the resulting computations necessarily more complex, intricate and error-prone.

Building 'awareness': a BIM system 'understands' that is it representing a building

In a BIM-based design workflow, building 'awareness' built into the data itself allows the architect to merely ask the system for each of these answers, all of which are inherent in the representation itself due to BIM's built-in capabilities, irrespective of level of detail or design phase. Changing the parameters of the design adjusts these data dynamically, with the accompanying increase in precision resulting in greater understanding and insight about the project since the model is 'aware' of its characteristics. An architect designing to a target space program, for example, sees that math as a result of the design representation itself rather than a separate process for which she is responsible. In this particular case, the outcome that the architect is working to satisfy is, on the one hand, conformance to the spatial brief, and on the other, adherence to the cost target. Providing the necessary computations to achieve these is considerably easier in a technology-enabled design context.

Representing construction logic

At the other end of the design process is the relationship of design intent to construction logic. Traditionally, architects are expected to be familiar with the approaches and techniques of construction, but are separated by contract and professional standards from involvement in its means and methods.[16] The builder, upon receipt of the architect's documents, has to figure out exactly what is required to construct the building, interpreting what the architect has chosen to depict and often interpolating between the technical assertions of the architect's production drawings and what is necessary to construct a physical building. Nowhere in the production documents are there any instructions with regard to construction sequence or logic, even when such insight is crucial to its assembly. An architect and her engineers may have decided, for example, that the structural frame of her building is concrete, although the tight urban site selected has no room for concrete trucks or the pumpers necessary to actually place the concrete on each floor. Perhaps a cast-in-place option would be more suitable for reasons of cost, availability or logistics, but this idea was foregone during conceptual design because the architect had no responsibility for that decision nor any understanding of the logistics implications of the choice of system.[17] Changing systems at the outset of construction means massive re-documentation, re-engineering and re-permitting, and thus such a change is not just impractical but almost impossible.

Increasingly robust representational models (through BIM and other means) are moving design and construction logic closer together, providing construction insight for the former directly from the latter as demonstrated in Figure 3.3.4. Analytical platforms that assess and recommend construction approaches can evaluate the construction implications of a designer's approach during any stage of the design from concept through production, making decisions more supportable across a wide range of construction implications, most importantly cost and schedule, the so-called "fourth dimen-

3.3.4

4D
construction planing

---

16 See AIA Standard Form of Agreement B101-2017, Section 3.6.1.2, which states: "The Architect shall not have control over, charge over, nor responsibility for the means, methods, techniques or procedures" of construction. These are the responsibility of the contractor.
17 The author recently learned of a project where an architect's decision to configure the ground floor plan incurred an additional $1 million in construction cost because of the difficulty of placing a crane on the site. Had that issue been anticipated in the original concept for the building, the project would have cost considerably less.

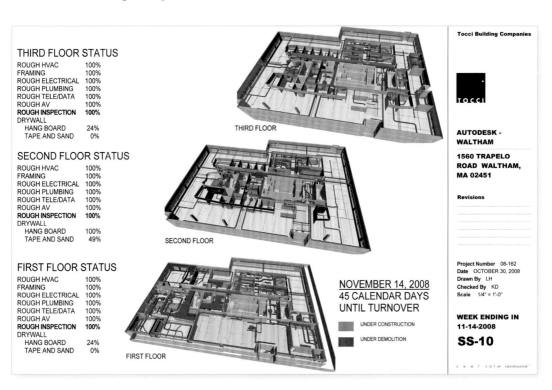

THIRD FLOOR STATUS

ROUGH HVAC	100%
FRAMING	100%
ROUGH ELECTRICAL	100%
ROUGH PLUMBING	100%
ROUGH TELE/DATA	100%
ROUGH AV	100%
ROUGH INSPECTION	**100%**
DRYWALL	
HANG BOARD	24%
TAPE AND SAND	0%

THIRD FLOOR

SECOND FLOOR STATUS

ROUGH HVAC	100%
FRAMING	100%
ROUGH ELECTRICAL	100%
ROUGH PLUMBING	100%
ROUGH TELE/DATA	100%
ROUGH AV	100%
ROUGH INSPECTION	**100%**
DRYWALL	
HANG BOARD	100%
TAPE AND SAND	49%

SECOND FLOOR

FIRST FLOOR STATUS

ROUGH HVAC	100%
FRAMING	100%
ROUGH ELECTRICAL	100%
ROUGH PLUMBING	100%
ROUGH TELE/DATA	100%
ROUGH AV	100%
ROUGH INSPECTION	**100%**
DRYWALL	
HANG BOARD	24%
TAPE AND SAND	0%

FIRST FLOOR

NOVEMBER 14, 2008
45 CALENDAR DAYS
UNTIL TURNOVER

UNDER CONSTRUCTION

UNDER DEMOLITION

Tocci Building Companies

AUTODESK -
WALTHAM

1560 TRAPELO
ROAD WALTHAM,
MA 02451

Revisions

Project Number 08-162
Date OCTOBER 30, 2008
Drawn By LH
Checked By KD
Scale 1/4" = 1'-0"

WEEK ENDING IN
11-14-2008

SS-10

c o o l c a l m constructed

sions" of representation. As the contractor's tools for planning schedule and sequence improve over time, they can be applied to an evolving design. This will be particularly evident as computational approaches become more prominent in the on-site processes of construction with automated tools, industrialized construction techniques and robotics, which will require a direct connection from design data to the field while simultaneously accumulating data about effectiveness that can be a feedback loop back to design decisions themselves. Integrated collaboration platforms connect builders directly to the design process as it unfolds, creating further process integration between design and construction, the inputs and outputs of an optimized result (see Chapters 3.4, "Building Logic and Design Intent," and 3.5, "Design Demands of Digital Making").

Generating alternatives by optimization

Just as design options can be represented and evaluated with these technologies, they can also be generated, *sui generis*, computationally. As I have described earlier (see Chapter 3.1, "Procedures, Process and Outcome"), the digitization of design information makes it accessible and manipulable by scripts and algorithms allowing the designer to create not just the direct design, but the decision-making context within which the design can be gener-

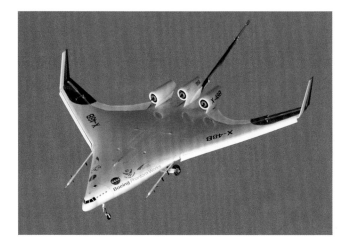

ated. Today's designers use scripts to manipulate the geometric characteristics of design (typically with geometry modelers like Rhino) but soon that same approach will be applied to the array of parameters made available by BIM. A design script could, for example, not just parametrically adjust the dimensions of a window, but size that window by changing the cooling capacity of the air conditioning system. Thus generating alternatives by algorithm expands the realm of possible solutions, and applying analytical engines to evaluate those options empowers a designer to examine a far greater range of opportunities while simultaneously demonstrating their efficacy and results.

These techniques have been employed in other disciplines. Aircraft designers have long used a process called multi-disciplinary design optimization (MDDO),[18] where mathematical techniques for finding optimal solutions in the intersection of several engineering constraints are generated and evaluated computationally. The latest generation of blended wing aircraft, as illustrated in Figure 3.3.5, resulted from such an approach, where structure, weight and aerodynamic properties were solved in concert rather than individually. Another strategy for computationally generated options is through genetic algorithms, which use principles of evolutionary biology to create, test, sort and propagate series of design solutions which are dynamically tested for fitness by accompanying analytical engines. Each approach blends a combination of traditional direct design manipulation, computa-

Multi-disciplinary design optimization (MDDO)

3.3.5

18 MDDO "is a field of engineering that uses optimization methods to solve design problems incorporating a number of disciplines. It is also known as multidisciplinary optimization and multidisciplinary system design optimization (MSDO)." See https://en.wikipedia.org/wiki/Multidisciplinary_design_optimization.

tionally generated options and analytic evaluation eventually yielding to newly empowered decision-making by the responsible designer.

Changes in expectations and obligations

These examples are early indications of the important shift in the nature of the design process. Computation both widens the range of possibilities of design and provides the means to evaluate and demonstrate the effectiveness of solutions. In concert, the various improvements in design technology mean that design decisions can be predicated upon analytic, and thereby predictable, results generated by the informational, analytical and collaborative infrastructure of computationally-enabled design, with profound implications. Professional judgment, as dispensed by architects, has often relied upon the experience, intuition and credibility of the architect, and success measured less by the ability to achieve transformational results than to meet the basic requirements of building performance, budgets and schedules. In the very near term, these more transactional, technical (and, dare we say, prosaic) aspects of design outcomes will be substantiated by computation, and results much more reliably presented. This means that architects can begin to organize their work, relationships with collaborators, and contractual commitments correlated not with commoditized fees or even based on hourly billing rates, but rather on the results produced by the architect's ideas — as opposed to the cost of production of design. Design generation (optioneering), solutions selection and optimization can be a result of both synthetic and analytic process (combining the designer's judgment with computationally generated options) and rewarded accordingly. And the increased effectiveness of decision-making in the technical aspects of design, which are those most likely to be computational in the near future, leave the architect more time and room to explore more complex answers to design questions, as I have suggested elsewhere.[19]

The structure and phasing of the design process as they relate to the overall systems of delivery are likely to change in response to these newfound capabilities. Both the definitions and boundaries of the traditional stages of design are the first to fall under the pressures of design and construction teams who can rapidly define and explore options and make decisions differently. The earliest evidence of this change was apparent as CAD became ubiquitous, allowing production teams to manage and organize drawings easily; the advent of construction management approaches that

Fast-tracking

overlapped the stages of design in so-called 'fast-tracked' scenarios emerged as a result. This was the first indication of the elimination of 'waterfall' design sequencing, and now the edges of design stages themselves are beginning

19 Phillip G. Bernstein, "Intention to Artifact," in *Digital Workflows in Architecture: Designing Design — Designing Assembly — Designing Industry* (Basel: Birkhäuser, 2012).

to blur. Certain project components — enclosure systems, structural frames, air systems — can be chosen early in a project design and then their detailed characteristics can be defined even as the rest of the building's concept is incomplete, creating design-to-procurement/installation paths that cut across traditional design staging. The need to place a steel mill order might, for example, organize a design process in a way that the structural system is resolved, detailed and ordered long before the balance of the building. Robust, detailed representation and analysis, combined with the tools to quickly deliver the resulting design information, 'pulls' this sequence from the traditional progression, but the ability to use modeling tools to manage the resulting process complexity makes the new approach possible and even desirable. The architect simply continues to design with this constraint in mind.

New systems of value

Integrated project delivery (IPD) and target value delivery

Project delivery methods like integrated project delivery (IPD) and target value delivery[20] are examples of new constellations of clients, designers and contractors that have emerged in response to both the challenges of a structurally inefficient building industry as well as the power of computational design and construction. These systems are characterized by a redefinition of the relationship of designers and builders, a reframing of the steps to define and achieve design/construction objectives, and new business models to allocate risk and reward. Unlike their predecessors (like Design Bid Build or Construction Management) they lay out protocols for carefully creating the measurable objectives of the design and construction process and use those metrics to both calibrate progress and reward (or punish) project participants accordingly. While the early versions of such ideas (particularly IPD) emerged from the assumption that model-based design was transparent enough to all the parties in order to enable better cooperation, these approaches are now increasingly based upon agreements that define project success. Correlating the strategic, business, operational and aspirational objectives of the client to both the design of the process and the design of the building itself makes outcome-based processes critical to the work of the architect, and, I would suggest, to the survival of the profession itself. With increasing pressures to build more complex projects faster, more precisely and with less money, the forces at play to improve construction are expanding, including automated construction and public/private capitalization of social infrastructure, to name a few. These forces are far larger than the influence of architects who wish to control them, and arming the profes-

---

20 Target Value Delivery is defined by the Lean Construction Institute as "(a) disciplined management practice to be used throughout the project to assure the facility meets the operational needs and values of the users, is delivered within the allowable budget, and promotes innovation through the process to increase value and eliminate waste." Kristen Hill, Katherine Copeland, Christian Pikel, *Target Value Delivery: Practitioner Guidebook to Implementation Current State 2016* (Arlington, VA: LEAN Construction Institute, 2016), p. 15.

sion of architecture with the ability to both create value and demonstrate that value through computation will assure the place of architects in the delivery systems of building in the future.

3.4

Building Logic and Design Insight

Is architectural design representation obliged to support and integrate into post-design activities such as construction and building operation, and if so, how does that affect design generation?

What are the appropriate outcomes of the act of architectural design? This question is often answered with a confusing array of comparisons and contrasts. Are architects artists or technicians? Conceptualizers or master builders? Only responsible for the 'intent' of the design or for seeing something through to an operating artifact? What is more important, the objectives of the commissioning client or the pursuit of a larger cultural agenda?[21]

'Architecture' and 'building'

Patrik Schumacher draws a distinction between 'Architecture' and 'building' where the former is about 'beauty and utility' and the latter about shelter.[22] He sees the function of the building itself as a critical component of architecture, and expression of that function manifests, in part, from the cultural agenda of the project. His firm's fascination with curvilinear forms derives directly from the desire to 'smooth' the spatial experience that is derived from the complex interaction of various functional forces that result from a cultural agenda, and the firm has developed enormous expertise in how to generate, detail, procure and build such forms.

3.4.1

Conflicts of concepts and construction

Peter Eisenman sees architecture as a "conceptual, cultural, and intellectual enterprise… [versus]… a phenomenological enterprise – that is, the experience of the subject in architecture, the experience of materiality, of light, of color, of space and etc."[23] Eisenman only engages in building itself in order to legitimize the intellectual objectives of his work but decides that "(a)rchitecture involves seeing whether those ideas can withstand the attack of building, of people, of time, of function, etc." He goes on to declare, "I couldn't care less"[24] about the

---

21 The design curator and theorist Paola Antonelli often describes design as "Art + Reality" (personal conversation with Brian Kenet, 6 March 2018).
22 Schumacher, Vienna IOA Silver Lecture.
23 Iman Ansari, "Eisenman's Evolution: Architecture, Syntax, and New Subjectivity," *Arch Daily* (2013).

3.4.1 Construction of Heydar Aliyev Center by Zaha Hadid Architects, Baku, Azerbaijan

3.4.2 phenomenological issues but hopes that he can narrow the gap between an intellectual construct and the physical result as much as possible.

So even at the extreme edge of architecture as a theoretical exercise, architects seem to need to build, if only to assure that their ideas can be seen at full scale and experienced. And as Manfredo Tafuri apparently once said to Eisenman: "Peter, if you don't build no one will take your ideas seriously. You have to build because ideas that are not built are simply ideas that are not built."[25] Of course, each architect has to choose where to invest that energy, and Eisenman (proudly, it seems) claims that only twenty-five of his hundred-and-fifty-odd projects have been constructed. One of the most important, the Aronoff Center in Cincinnati, is considered both a theoretical and experiential tour-de-force. But when its exterior envelope failed only fourteen years after its completion, he seemed completely uninterested in being involved in its renewal, acceding only to a conversation with the technical architects who had proposed changing the exterior colors during the renovation.[26] Being taken seriously apparently only goes so far, especially when the statute of limitations (the time period within which the architect

3.4.3 can be sued for negligence) has run out.

24 Ibid.
25 Ibid.
26 Lawrence Biemiller, "At 14, Iconic Building at U. of Cincinnati Is Already a Candidate for Preservation," *The Chronicle of Higher Education* (2010).

3.4.2 The City of Culture in Santiago de Compostela, Spain by Eisenman Architects

If we buy Schumacher's argument about architecture as an "autopoietic"[27] social enterprise, it needs strong theoretical platforms to evolve, innovate and remain culturally relevant as well as useful. But to realize that relevance architects must also build, and thereby cannot avoid their responsibility to look across the execution and efficacy gaps between intent, construction and occupancy. Therefore, even for architects most deeply engaged in the intellectual pursuits of Architecture writ large, there is a direct responsibility to understand how their buildings are created and used. As I will argue later (see Chapter 4.4, "New Values in the Systems of Delivery"), this is a critical component of not just remaining relevant but increasing the real value of architects in society.

Three questions of intent and execution

Consider three important questions that must be faced by the architect who wants to see her work built. First, does she have an understanding of performance of building materials and systems and the implications of their inclusion in the project? This might be considered basic 'table stakes' for any competent architect. Second, can she depict the project in a form that both accomplishes her design intent and respects the means and methods of

27 "Autopoieisis" is a system "capable of reproducing and maintaining itself," Wikipedia at https://en.wikipedia.org/wiki/Autopoiesis; see also p. 66.

modern construction? And third, since clients depend on architects to translate scarce resources (capital) into physical objects (buildings), can the architect be a responsible steward of costs? At the risk of flinging the architect's theoretical aspirations into the operational mire, these issues are the most directly problematic since a majority of lawsuits emerge (filed by either clients or builders) alleging failures to properly answer them, along with a litany of accompanying complaints about the results.[28]

Failure to deliver results   The industry itself does not enjoy a particularly good reputation for delivering those three results. Broader metrics like "35% of industry resources are wasted"[29] are further substantiated by the track record in the field, where most projects fail to meet their budgets or schedules, at least here in the United States, with 93% of owners reporting late schedules, and 85% reporting budget misses.[30] Some responsibility must be borne here by clients who set up projects badly before any architect or contractor is on the scene, but once those contracts are let, about a third of projects fail to meet these im-

28 See "Let's Stop Letting Starchitects Ruin College Campuses" at https://www.pps.org/blog/starchitects-and-campuses/.

29 Sir John Egan, *Rethinking Construction: Report of the Construction Task Force to the Deputy Prime Minister* (Department of Trade and Ministry, 1998).

30 Dodge Data and Analytics (ed.), "Optimizing the Owner Organization: The Impact of Policies and Practices on Performance" (New York: Dodge, 2016), http://analyticsstore.construction.com/OptimizingOwnerOrg.html.

portant objectives.[31] A recent study concluded that, on any given construction site on a given day, most future work is almost certain to be either late or early — and neither is an efficient way to build.[32] Construction projects have a well-deserved reputation for being unpredictable, painful, unprofitable and litigious. Hardly a good way to spend $10 trillion a year, worldwide.[33]

For architects building today responding to all three of these questions is increasingly challenging and complex. A bewildering array of materials and construction systems are available through the global industry supply chain, and understanding their use is not just a limited question of finish or cost but also includes implications for the global carbon economy, the energy consumption of the building in which they are to be installed as well as their ability to weather, resist water and be maintained. They may be prefabricated offsite or assembled in place. They will interact with other systems in the building, resulting in unintended consequences. In the transition from design specification to selection and installation, the contractor — who has the same digitally enabled access to enormous databases of alternatives — may recommend a cheaper or more efficient alternative to a given selection or system, increasing the complexity of the decision-making process further. An architect who willingly ignores this dizzying array of choices is at best deferring her responsibilities, and at worst, negligent.

Ends versus means, design and outcomes

Architects' models and drawings (the instruments of service) are a static representation of the proposed 'end state' of construction, varying in their levels of abstraction, fidelity and detail relative to the final constructed building. But construction is a dynamic process that relies heavily on an understanding of sequence, assembly logic as well as complex orchestration of labor, materials and delivery — not to mention cash flow. Traditional delivery approaches in Western construction delegate the entire responsibility for figuring this stuff out to the builder, despite the fact that significant decisions about same are made, *a priori,* by the designer by virtue of her choices, often long before any builder is in the picture. If design thinking precedes construction thinking entirely, the likelihood of success — measured strictly in terms of budget, schedule, quality and margin — is clearly limited. So, while one could parse the legal particulars, the architect's design intent implies a lot about the means and methods of design. The intent should reflect the same design outcomes at minimum, but instantiating the logic of con-

31 Harvey M. Bernstein, "Managing Uncertainty and Expectations in Building Design and Construction."
32 M. Fischer and M. Schutz, "Construction Planning and Feedback Loops – Analysis of Current Practice," in *Stanford Center for Facilities Engineering Technical Advisory Committee* (Palo Alto, CA: Stanford University, 2017).
33 McKinsey Global Institute (ed.), "Reinventing Construction: A Route to Higher Productivity," (McKinsey & Company, 2017), https://www.mckinsey.com/industries/capital-projects-and-infrastructure/our-insights/reinventing-construction-through-a-productivity-revolution, p.vi. See http://marketreportsstore.com/global-construction-outlook-2020/.

struction might be part of more modern instruments of service. Firms with a deep interest in making — like New York's SHoP Architects or Gluck+ — have begun to change their documents accordingly. SHoP will often define the fabrication and assembly sequence of its buildings, and Gluck+, who build the projects they design, have forsaken traditional 'discipline-based' documents (like 'the architectural drawings,' 'the structural drawings' and so forth), going directly to trade-based documents that directly describe the work of each sub-contractor and trade package.

3.4.4

Design intent, construction materiality, the means and methods of construction, management, planning and logic, and market conditions are the complex stew that comprises construction cost estimating, perhaps one of the most daunting (and ineffective) responsibilities of architecture and building. And while computers have helped with the elemental components of any estimate like counts and quantities, accurate cost estimating — in the rare instances when it happens, usually with outside cost estimators — is as much art as science. Nonetheless, standard contracts require architects to estimate costs as part of their services, stipulating that:

> (T)he Cost of the Work shall be the total cost to the Owner to construct all elements of the Project designed or specified by the Architect and shall include contractors' general conditions costs, overhead and profit... Evaluations of the Owner's budget for the Cost of

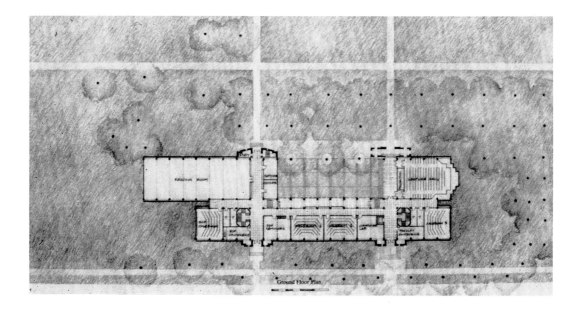

Ground Floor Plan

the Work, the preliminary estimate of the Cost of the Work and updated estimates of the Cost of the Work prepared by the Architect, represent the Architect's judgment as a design professional. It is recognized, however, that neither the Architect nor the Owner has control over the cost of labor, materials or equipment; the Contractor's methods of determining bid prices; or competitive bidding, market or negotiating conditions. Accordingly, the Architect <u>cannot and does not warrant or represent that bids or negotiated prices will not vary from the Owner's budget</u> (emphasis added) for the Cost of the Work...[34]

Hardly a ringing endorsement of the architect's ability to project costs and protect the Owner's valuable capital. Is this just architects trying to escape responsibility for likely budget busts, or is this a signal of a larger issue like a lack of expertise or missed expectations? And if so, what should be done?

Remediating strategies

3.4.5

Up through the 1980s, a few hand-drawn documents, an honest and experienced builder, and a handshake agreement to cooperate delivered a building, and the execution gap was narrow. Figure 3.4.5 is a hand-drawn floor plan of an award-winning building designed in 1980 that required less than one

34 American Institute of Architects, *B101-2017 Standard Form of Agreement between Owner and Architect* (Washington, DC: American Institute of Architects, 2017), Section 6.3, p. 15.

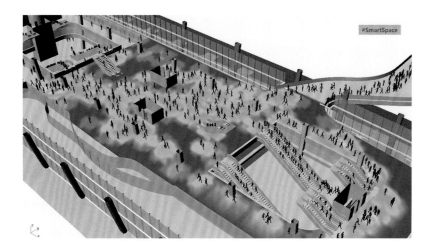

hundred sheets of documents to build. But the profession today has only two strategies to relate to construction: separation, or integration. Separation — distancing from responsibility for things like cost or schedule — is a product of attempts to shield the limited profit margins of practice from the vagaries of litigation. Construction costs are an indicator of performance health across all three of our challenge questions, and thus it is logical to assume that architects would wish to distance themselves from this dangerous responsibility, particularly one so dependent on the actions and decisions of another player like the contractor, with whom such relationships vary from mild distrust to outright hostility.

I would argue that the separation strategy has yielded little gain or profit in the last forty years, and an integrative approach is more promising. It is here where the opportunities of modern technology step into the breach, where architects might remediate the broken relationship with construction with new flows of information and insight. As representations of an emergent design become more digitally robust, there is an enormous amount of information useful to a contractor no matter when they join the project; precise geometry, three-dimensional models, annotative metadata about building elements all provide much higher fidelity information supporting much better decision-making. These are the benefits of increased data flow from the architect to the builder.

But the opposite direction is equally important: as construction managers, sub-contractors and product manufacturers create digital information about their systems, procedures and uses of materials, that information can and should be accessed by architects to improve insights across the three questions (systems, representation and costs), improve the originating

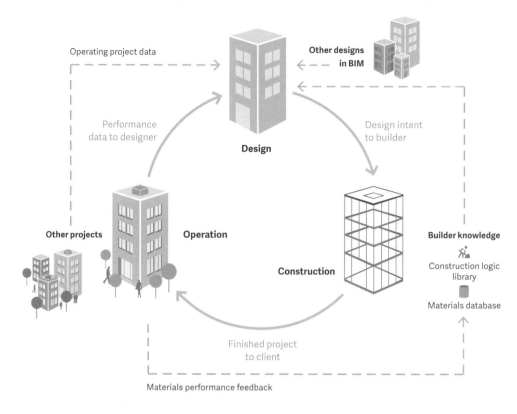

ideas of design, and make predicted outcomes of construction more likely. Both sides of the execution gap should thus work to make such exchanges as useful as possible, and act in the interest of the project rather from their own defensive postures (and profit margins).

Building operations   The architect's relationship to building 'operations' — or rather, how the building is occupied, used and maintained — should be less troublesome. A competent design should anticipate and define these things as a matter of course, particularly as regards the building's use. Schumacher argues that an understanding and instantiation of these social patterns is a necessary parameter of the design itself. The bi-directional paths on which information flows between designer and builder are no less important than those between designer and building user or operating system, and these paths are paved by information technology. Predictive analysis during design today really only includes systems operations like heating, cooling or energy, but emerging simulative tools that can anticipate human interaction and behavior in the space are not far behind, and in fact are already in use for escape simulations (by fire engineers) and for creating the behavior of large crowds of people via computer graphics in movies and video games. Data

accumulated about these same uses (from energy to behavior), collected by sensor systems integrated into the building, generates an enormous reference set against which future designs can be tested. As data collection from existing buildings — through technologies like laser scanning and photographic reality capture — augments the database for operations, the platform for cataloguing and understanding 'what was tried' versus 'what actually worked' will expand to support future design approaches.

3.4.6, 3.4.7

The opportunities of these integration strategies are obvious, *prima facie*. But for them to be fully realized requires architects to consider, design and implement more than just new workflows or advanced computational tools applied to digital data. All the players in the building industry — clients, designers and constructors — operate in large systems of capital, supply chains, and legal/political protocols. The constructs under which projects are organized — usually called project delivery models — establish the roles, responsibilities, relationships, risks and exchanges of value that form a system within which a building is realized. Theoretical design aspirations, opportunities to smooth information flows, improvements in insight, data gathering and analysis — none of these things is possible without proper improvements in the overall systems of delivery themselves.

Project delivery models

Design instruments and results

There was a time, as computer-aided drafting was becoming more widespread (early 1990s), where low profit margins and the high cost of buying CAD software, hardware and training gave architects the opportunity to implement the tool and charge for it by the hour, adding 'CAD Operations' expense to their invoices. Over time, owners saw these tools fully integrated into practice and refused to pay for them, as the benefits of their use did not accrue to them but rather the designers themselves: faster, more efficient and accurate drawings. Lawsuits, however, did not decrease despite the explosion of defensive drafting that CAD made possible. Fast-forward to the present, when these same architects are creating data-rich building information models with lots of potential to improve both construction and building outcomes and use. The value of the information complex and related process improvements of technology-driven design and construction are apparent, but not realizable unless the increase in value to everyone changes the system of delivery. Better results should mean less risk and higher profits for all, and create the real motivations for architects to connect more deeply to the systems and responsibilities of construction and building operation. To give away the first advantages of these models, like their CAD predecessors, is to mortgage the future of the profession itself.

It's therefore necessary to examine, deconstruct and reform the systems of project delivery in concert with the adoption of the possibilities of new technology. That reform is less reliant on the specifics of tools but rather with disassociating all aspects of building — design, construction and operation — from commodification, assets 'purchased' by clients by arbitraging and privileging lowest costs at the expense (literally) of everything else. Experiments in new delivery abound today: in relational contracting (like integrated project delivery); architects as fabricators (with SHoP Architects as a famous example); and architects expanding to delivery projects from financing through operation.

A provocative example of such an approach can be found in the Brooklyn, New York firm Alloy Development. Comprised of approximately twenty architects, Alloy is a self-contained 'building eco-system', that searches for development projects, procures land, assembles financing, designs the necessary building to their own specifications and then builds, sells or

A self-contained 'building eco-system'

rents, and operates their projects. All the challenges, opportunities and profits redouble to the firm itself, which uses advanced data collection and analysis to choose and evaluate projects and measure their performance. The firm 'contracts with itself' to provide all the necessary services to complete the project, often signing contracts where both parties are principals of the firm. This is an example of the complete decommoditization of the design/build process in the interest of maximum control and value creation. Needless to say, the firm is very profitable, nimble and, according to the principals, happy.

3.4.8

What differentiates Alloy and their fellow process innovators is their intensive focus on design and construction services as outcomes with specific purposes, and not commodities purchased in the stunted exchanges of traditional delivery models. If the systems of value creation, as aptly demonstrated in the extreme by Alloy, based on project outcomes and not lowest possible prices, can be changed, architects have both the means and the advantages to bridge both the execution and efficacy gaps, and should so with enthusiasm.

3.5

Design Demands of Digital Making

How do new means of physical production affect practice?

When Alberti first separated the act of design from that of building, he demanded precise fidelity between the architect's instructions and the builder's result,[35] presuming that information provided by the architect would be completely sufficient for the task. Analog design and building deployed the abstraction strategy of orthographic projection produced via drawing, which was, along with a lot of conversation, the primary vector between conception and execution. The intervening five hundred years, however, saw the emergence of a yawning gap between the disciplines of design and construction as buildings became more complex, practitioners more specialized, construction materials and techniques more involved and risk and liability concerns paramount. Nostalgia notwithstanding, the romantic ideal of the Master Builder has, by necessity, been largely left behind.

Making ambivalence   Even so, the architect's ambivalent relationship with making is a relatively recent phenomenon. Vitruvius, in the last of the *Ten Books on Architecture*, takes pains to explain the machinery by which buildings are to be constructed,[36] and the elemental definitions of buildings that precede this final chapter include detailed instructions for how to fabricate and transport columns, architraves and other components. As stated by Henry Petroski describing the close spacing of columns in the classical orders:

> *Concerns about aesthetics and buildability were often inseparable...*
> *the distance horizontally between the adjacent vertical supports*
> *could only be made so long before they would crack and break under*
> *the burden of their own considerable weight, either during the pro-*

---

35 See chapter 2.2, "Defining Design Intent, Precision and Results," and Carpo, *The Alphabet and the Algorithm*, p. 21.

36 The Ten Books were originally only text; subsequent authors generated drawings from Vitruvius's descriptions as shown in Figure 3.5.1.

cess of being lifted into place or after the additional weight of friezes and pediments was placed upon them.[37]

Design was a function of not just expressive intent, but also installation strategy.

3.5.1

In the early twentieth century, the operational separation between architects and builders was more a matter of contractual convenience than a division of labor between designing and making. Shreve, Lamb & Harmon, architects of the Empire State Building in New York City, employed more than two hundred construction supervisors to direct the build of that skyscraper, working hand-in-hand with the contractors, Starrett Brothers and Eken[38] during what were perhaps the last throes of meaningful collaborative relationships between designers and builders. The liability crisis of the 1980s and 1990s drove a wedge between them that lasts until today, manifest in various constellations of conventional project delivery that strive to exempt the various players from liability for the pitfalls of increasingly complex and litigious construction. Nothing is more emblematic of the current divide than the stricture that appears in standard form contracts by the American Institute of Architects, which state unambiguously:

3.5.1 Cesar Cesarino's
Drawing of Vitruvius

> *The Architect shall not have control over, <u>charge of, or responsibility for the construction means, methods, techniques, sequences or procedures</u> (emphasis added), or for the safety precautions and programs in connection with the Work, nor shall the Architect have responsibility for the Contractor's failure to perform the Work in accordance with the requirements of the Contract Documents.*[39]

Harvard's Rafael Moneo described this fissure in even more stark terms:

> *The intimacy between architecture and construction has been broken. This intimacy was once the very nature of the architectural work and somehow was always manifested in its appearance... To be an architect, therefore, has traditionally implied being a builder; that is, explaining to others how to build. The knowledge (when not the mastery) of the building techniques was always implicit in the idea of producing architecture... Architects in the past were both architects and*

37 Henry Petroski, *To Forgive Design: Understanding Failure* (Cambridge, MA: Belknap Press of Harvard University Press, 2012), p. 34, and Pollio Vitruvius and M. H. Morgan, *Vitruvius: The Ten Books on Architecture* (New York: Dover Publications, 1960), p. 80.

38 For an excellent description of the construction of the Empire State Building, see Neal Bascomb, *Higher: A Historic Race to the Sky and the Making of a City* (New York: Doubleday, 2003).

39 American Institute of Architects, *B101-2017 Standard Form of Agreement between Owner and Architect*, Section 3.6.1.2, p. 8.

builders. Before the present disassociation, the invention of form was also the invention of its construction. One implied the other.[40]

The architect may define the intent of the final result through her drawings and specifications, but the route to getting to that end is strictly the contractor's job, at least in America. In other places (like, for example, Brazil) the architect has little or no role in construction, handing over documents and hoping that the project is built in some rough approximation of what has been designed. In Japan, the design handed to the builder is intentionally incomplete, and the final details are worked out together, while in Germany

3.3.2 the architect's scope of work extends to building operation. (See Figure 3.3.2 which provides a comparison of the architect's services in major construction economies.)

Opportunities of the computational turn

Both sides of this divide are transforming in the second digital turn, as is their relationship.

Design is increasingly reliant on modeling, simulation, analysis and data-intensive 'reality capture' of existing physical context, creating a rich source of precise reference information with potential to inform and improve construction. Three-dimensional digital models, for example, represent full-scale virtual replicas of the buildings they presage. Computational analysis makes these models excellent platforms for predicting building assembly, construction, operation and performance. As modeling and simulative tools become more capable, they will represent not just the final, assembled artifact of the building, but the underlying logic and performance by which the buildings come together and, eventually, behave. Over time, libraries of such models will be indexed and accessible by machine learning algorithms that will extract protocol norms and best practice, making them widely available to both designers and builders.

Construction, once exclusively reliant on either human or hydraulic production, is now slowly automating. Computer numerically controlled (CNC) fabrication is moving from the factory floor to the job site. A raft of other digital technologies promises to nudge construction into the modern age, including robotics, high-resolution reality capture of physical conditions, new digitally created high-performance materials and building systems, application of big data to construction analytics and a wide array of computer-assisted supply chain management and assembly techniques. As designers and builders become digital and data drives machines, they will become increasingly reliant upon one another, and the means-and-methods divide will begin to close when digital information traverses that divide. What

---

40 Rafael Moneo, *The Solitude of Buildings: Kenzo Tange Lecture* (Cambridge, MA: Harvard Graduate School of Design, 1985).

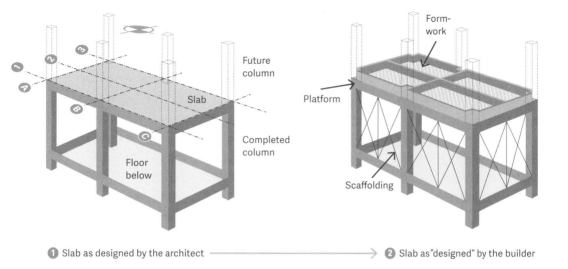

① Slab as designed by the architect ⟶ **②** Slab as "designed" by the builder

does this bridge mean for the designer and design process? And what systemic influences might convert this obvious opportunity into actual changes in the relationship between the designer and the builder?

Industry optimization

The ineffectiveness of the building industry itself is a good place to start. Concerns about the productivity of the building supply chain are well established and pre-date even the earliest efforts to digitize design and construction. As early as 1965, research on the challenges of the industry suggested that:

> *The basic decisions of construction control are often incomplete or unduly rushed because necessary information is not available sufficiently ahead of time, or is not complete enough. On many occasions members of the construction team could, but do not, ease this problem by supplying the data that would facilitate the preparation of fuller and more useful information by others. Building construction is remarkable among industrial activities for the lack of detailed information about how it proceeds.*[41]

It is not just an unwillingness to exchange information that Higgin identifies, but its incompatibility for use across the various phases of design and construction that inhibits transparent, clear and efficient interaction between the architects, engineers and builders. Since the designers have no respon-

41 Gurth Higgin, William Neil Jessop and Tavistock Institute of Human Relations London, *Communications in the Building Industry; the Report of a Pilot Study*, 2nd ed. (London: Tavistock Publications, 1965).

sibility for construction means and methods, their outputs describe, mostly in general terms, the final result of the construction process without a lot of regard for the necessary steps to achieve them. So even if the architect were willing to provide the builder with her digital drawings, they must be recast in a form useful in the field. Each player sees the question differently, as described in Figure 3.5.2.

By way of example, let us look at the example of the concrete slabs that comprise the floors of most large buildings. The architect and design structural engineer will describe that slab as a large, continuous piece of concrete that runs from building edge to edge. The concrete subcontractor, however, must determine exactly how to pour that concrete, likely in lifts that are a function of the available form work and concrete pumping capacity, location and reach. The subcontractor subdivides the pour into 'chunks' that conform to that plan, including the approach for deploying and reusing the forms, creating its own strategy for construction. This subcontractor must convert design intent to something that more accurately reflects the logic of its construction strategy. Essentially, both parties remodel the building to their own ends, introducing inefficiencies in the process (the owner pays for both representations), and opportunities for error.

Design methodology changes

As construction becomes increasing digitally mechanized, this strange divide makes less and less sense. Design must be more deeply informed by making, and vice versa. Architects have pioneered techniques in the intersection of controlled geometry, parametric form generation and digital fabrication, which suggests that perhaps there are new opportunities to come. Use of digital fabrication equipment has been standard in most schools of architecture for at least a decade, and it has been argued that architects largely created the idea of mass customization — that each computer-manufactured copy of a produced artifact can be adjusted uniquely by adjusting the production parameters that control the producing machine.[42] Of course, the physical results of this profound idea, at least in building, have largely been the formal exuberance of the "Blobmeisters" despite Schumacher's exhortations to the contrary (see Chapter 3.1, "Procedures, Processes and Outcome", for a deeper exploration). Perhaps today, the route to connecting design intent and building performance travels via construction, with four immediate and inter-related opportunities for design to evolve:

1. Representational resolution One of the original promises of BIM was its alleged ubiquitous utility across the design and construction process. The thinking here was obvious, if flawed: a three-dimensionally robust, behavior-

---

42 Carpo, *The Second Digital Turn: Design Beyond Intelligence.*

ally integrated representation of the asset would be helpful in both creating a complete design and transmitting its particulars to the builder with clarity. While it may be true that BIM-based design deliverables are more accurate and complete than their CAD-generated predecessors,[43] they can often be more abstract and conceptual than detailed, leaving the builder to fill in the blanks. Construction documents — the primary medium of exchange between the architect and builder — are still diagrams of the very complex building asset they are meant to describe, a product of traditional procedures, the standard of care and feeble attempts to assign the risk of construction to the builder. They are, by these traditions, notional, abstract and low fidelity. As proficiency with 3D modeling increases,[44] designers in adventuresome firms looking to build complex forms have extracted geometric control information from their design models (usually in the form of spreadsheets of X|Y|Z coordinates) and transmitted same to digital fabricators, who otherwise would be required to generate buildable geometry from the general dimensions typical of architectural working drawings. But that precision alone has been the extent of the benefits enjoyed by a builder from the digital turn.

The potential of cloud-based modeling tools allows the designer to explore, interrogate, refine and represent the design at much higher levels of resolution and performance. This could yield the obvious result of transmitting higher resolution and higher fidelity information across the design-construction chasm. Builders have demanded CAD files — and the full-scale geometry they contain — from designers since CAD was first in use, precisely because of the obvious efficiencies of not having to reconstruct and verify it prior to construction. Digitized design means that the combination of more powerful modeling tools and a wider availability of digital product data about materials, building elements and pre-assembled systems will, understandably, whet that appetite further.

2. Assembly logic Digital models extend the representational capabilities of a pre-built design to the logic of assembly and construction. The so-called 'fourth dimension' of CAD — time — is more than just marking 3D model assemblies in sequence in a BIM-based project. Algorithmic overlays to the representation itself can memorialize not just the final result of construction, but the necessary steps of fabrication, assembly and installation. Architects are already using gaming engines for high-resolution representation,[45] but the ability to digitally simulate a construction process using simulative technology (not unlike a video game) will inevitably develop. Builders will 're-

4D: the 'fourth dimension'

43 Harvey M. Bernstein, "Managing Uncertainty and Expectations in Building Design and Construction."
44 It is not unusual today, however, for architects to mark their design BIM information with the proviso "not for construction."
45 For an excellent example, see the visualization team at HKS at http://www.archengine.org/.

cord' construction techniques and standards through such simulations, making them available for designers to reference as they consider certain construction systems. Product manufacturers, eager for their stuff to be specified by designers and purchased by builders, will incorporate the digital fabrication constraints and parameters in the digital product information available during selection.

The information flow will start from the builder and manufacturer and lead to the designer, making building logic accessible as a consideration for the architect. Eventually, however, as designers master this constraint, the information flow may well reverse again as newer, more daring and logically specific assembly techniques and systems are generated as innovative architectural solutions. The logic of construction in these cases will be a prerequisite to understanding and building the design, and therefore will be instantiated into the models that represent it.

3. Materials and systems performance Architects have always faced a bewildering array of choices of building products, materials and systems when specifying the particulars of a project. Every product comes with performance information — often transcribed as requirements into the project specifications by an architect with lots of experience in such matters. But how do we know if that curtain wall, door assembly, flashing detail or joint compound is up to snuff, if the lesser cost alternative offered by the contractor is actually equivalent to that which we specified, or if the interaction of those choices will lead to an unwelcome leak or other failure?

At one level, the ability to find, sort, analyze and select materials and systems is regularized by the digital approach, particularly one supported by the taxonomy of a building information model. BIM tools demand a consistency of representation and, at least in theory, a degree of completeness that lessens the chances for overt omission of a required building component. At the next level, BIM and accompanying analytical software give the designer the chance to simulate the implications of product choices before their penultimate installation; today's BIM-based energy analysis tools, for example, will predict the demands of heating and cooling loads based upon the choice of glass in a curtain wall (see Figure 3.5.3). While today manufacturers compete for the architect's attention with BIM-based content downloaded from their product websites, they are increasingly providing analytical tools like PPG's Vitro Glass evaluator[46] to encourage proper selection — and, of course, purchase as seen in Figure 3.5.4.[47]

3.5.3

PPG's Vitro Glass
evaluator, 3.5.4

---

46 http://www.vitroglazings.com/en-US/Resources/Tools-Design-Resources/Calculation-Tools.aspx.
47 Vitro Glass of PPG provides web-based tools for selection, construction, stress and energy analysis of their products,
    as can been seen at http://www.vitroglazings.com/en-US/Resources/Tools-Design-Resources/Calculation-Tools.aspx.

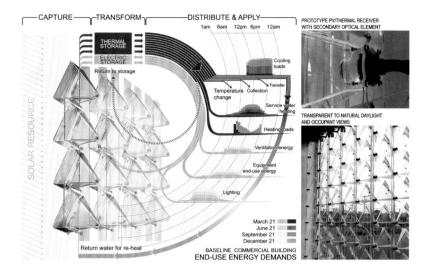

Adding to the world's collection of big data, digital design and performance information will accumulate over time and correlate to the specific experiences of projects performing in the field. Eventually the building industry will come to learn from such data to predict the reliability of products and systems, in a context where the 'science of computation' augments human experience as described by Mario Carpo:

> *What is today already a reality in the case of user-generated data (which is simply kept after use, and never discarded) may extend to the monitoring and tracking of all kinds of physical and material phenomena, such as the functioning of an engine, the bending of a skyscraper under wind loads, or global and local weather patterns.*[48]

Such an approach will certainly include the vagaries of product performance in a range of specific conditions, presuming the industry can find the wherewithal to leverage it.

4. Delivery control The opportunities described above are methodological, focused on the particular procedural options that might be available to cross the divide between design and making with the digital. But there is a final category that falls beyond the specifics of tools and into the realm of the systems of delivery where the architect participates. The dynamics of mod-

48 Mario Carpo, "The Alternative Science of Computation," *e-flux architecture*, "Artificial Labor," no. 23 (June 2017).

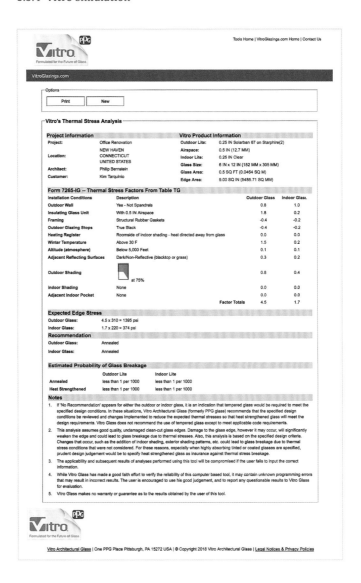

ern design and construction methods described in the beginning of this chapter currently circumscribe — and in many cases dramatically limit — the architect's influence and control over construction. Seen in one way, this makes sense: making buildings is a very complex enterprise, and everyone best 'mind their own position' on the field of play where a project is delivered. But in another, the division of labor between design and construction has stunted both and, in doing so, made adversaries of the actors to no good end: design and construction are inefficient, risky, only marginally profitable and sometimes very little fun. It has been this way for almost a century now. These conditions make the possibilities of transformation catalyzed by digi-

Opportunity	Design intent only	Intent + Execution
Representational resolution	Abstraction and diagrams, arbitrary focus on specific details	At the level of resolution needed for the builder to understand and build it without extensive re-elaboration
Assembly logic	A general understanding with no responsibility for means and methods	Design is informed by assembly logic provided by builders and manufacturer about their specific building elements.
Material performance	Provided by specifications and experience.	Performance parameters are provided as data accompanying the specification that can be part of analysis and predictive use.
Delivery control	Architects design, builders build.	Architects and builders cooperate on design-to-construction issues to optimize results.[50]

tal tools ripe, where the process of designing a building actually supports and enables that of construction, and Alberti's suggestion about "sound advice and clear drawings" is a two-way street between the architect and builder. The architect's roles, risks and responsibilities transform accordingly.

Integrated project delivery (IPD)

The emergent model called integrated project delivery (see Chapters 4.1, "Creating New Value Through Design," and 4.3, "Calibrating Design Values," for more information)[49] in the United States is a specific example of such evolution. This approach binds the designer, builder and client together with a single contract that eliminates the functional obligations of specific parties in opposition and tasks an entire team with achieving a set of measurable goals. Using the informational transparency of BIM — allowing everyone to understand progress clearly — design and construction objectives are concordant with those of the owner, including (for example) schedule and budget conformance, sustainability ratings and design quality. IPD as a construct continues to evolve, but the principles on which the approach is founded are key to closing the intent to execution gap, to wit: aligning everyone's efforts around accomplishing the overall goals of the project rather than division of labor connected to assignment of blame. This is an important, and likely first, bridge across this unfortunate divide.

3.5.5

49 Martin Fischer et al., *Integrating Project Delivery* (Hoboken, NJ: John Wiley & Sons, Inc., 2017).
50 Worth noting at this juncture that social and cultural norms in Japan have made this proposed relationship — which really is intended for Western building professionals — possible without technology. In general, designers and builders in Japan have a long history of close, non-confrontational cooperation, which is one reason that BIM has had a slow uptake in Japan, since the advantages of informational integration to enhance collaboration is not seen as necessary. For a more detailed description of the history and dynamics of the Japanese building industry, see Dana Buntrock, *Japanese Architecture as a Collaborative Process: Opportunities in a Flexible Construction Culture* (London, New York: Spon Press, 2001).

4

value

4.1

Creating New Value Through Design

How is value created in normative practice through scopes of service and deliverables and how does this change?

Each year in the United States, architects design and deliver, with their construction partners, approximately $400 billion in buildings, charging their clients about $30 billion in net fees.[1] With the likely exception of the single family dwelling you might live in, chances are that each day you visit and use a building designed by an architect. Those services are provided by approximately 110,000 licensed architects in the US.[2] In 2016, the average starting salary of a young architect in her first job in the profession ranged between $40,000 and $60,000 depending on firm size, experience and education, and after five years that range rises to $67,000 $85,000.[3] Architects are a relatively rare commodity in the US, with one architect for approximately every 3,000 people in the country. Although hardly a precise indicator of productivity, the ratio of fees paid to licensed practitioners in the US is about $250,000:1.

Lawyers play an analogous role in society in that they are professionals who are highly educated, certified and provide advice and counsel to clients about complex technical circumstances for which clients need help. According to the American Bar Association, there are approximately 1.3 million attorneys[4] in the United States (about one lawyer for every 40 people), whose starting salaries range between $54,000 to $139,000 (with some top graduates earning as much as $190,000) and five-year salaries ranging from $74,000 to $219,000.[5] The ratios at the top end of these ranges between young architects and lawyers are almost three to one.

1 "Net fees" are those retained by the firm and not paid to engineers, consultants or for reimbursable expenses like travel." Kermit Baker, Jennifer Riskus et al., *AIA Firm Survey Report: The Business of Architecture 2016* (Washington, DC: American Institute of Architects, 2016), p. 16.
2 National Council of Architectural Registration Boards (NCARB), "NCARB by the Numbers" (Washington, DC, 2016), p. 6.
3 Kermit Baker, Jennifer Riskus et al., *Compensation Report 2017* (Washington, DC: American Institute of Architects, 2017).
4 Matt Leicher to The Last Gen X American, 23 March 2016, https://lawschooltuitionbubble.wordpress.com/original-research-updated/lawyers-per-capita-by-state/.
5 Internet Legal Research Group, "Salaries of Legal Professionals 2016 (USA)" (2016), https://www.ilrg.com/employment/salaries/.

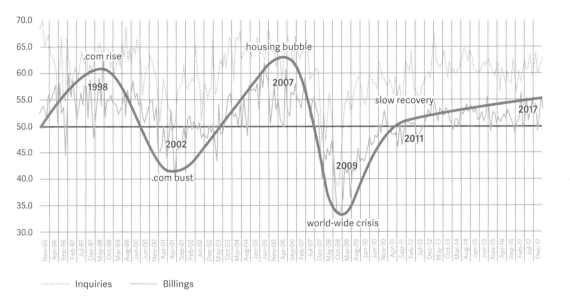

Inquiries .... Billings ———

These depressing numbers for architects are less a function of the actual value delivered to the economy by each respective profession than a failure by architects (and the business models of their practices) to convert that
value to compensation and profit. The peculiarities of that value conversion
have made architects particularly susceptible to the vagaries of the economy.

Economics and uncertain returns

The architecture profession has always been beset with economic uncertainty. In 2012, at the end of the great economic crisis, *The New York Times*
counseled "Want a Job? Go to College and Don't Major in Architecture,"[6] as
prospects for recent graduates at that juncture were so grim. Just three
short years later things had already turned around to the point that some
architects in New York, searching for talent to replenish their emaciated
staffs, complained that "(t)his is the toughest hiring market I've seen in twenty years."[7] At this writing in 2018, demand for architectural staff continues
unabated. The financial roller coaster is nothing new to practice, as the industry economic cycle moves up and down in regular five-to-seven-year cycles with macro-economic trends, buffeted by the capital markets, housing
4.1.1   finance and commercial demand, as illustrated in Figure 4.1.1, which tracks
monthly billing dynamics (with a baseline of 50.0).

6   Catherine Rampell, "Want a Job? Go to College, and Don't Major in Architecture," *The New York Times* (5 January
    2012), https://economix.blogs.nytimes.com/2012/01/05/want-a-job-go-to-college-and-dont-major-in-architecture/.
7   Erik Ipsen, "So Many Projects, So Few Architects. How Design Firms Are Filling a Talent Gap," *Crain's New York
    Business* (15 June 2015), http://www.crainsnewyork.com/article/20150615/REAL_ESTATE/150619936/so-many-
    projects-so-few-architects-how-design-firms-are-filling-a-talent-gap.

Firm profit margins, based on earnings before interest, bonus and taxes

Under 10%	Weak operating margin
10%–15%	Typical for most design firms
15%–20%	High margin firm, above average
20–25%	Top performing firm, unusual margins
Above 25%	Very rare, extraordinary performer

4.1.2

Most firms operate with a simple business model that receives fees from clients and converts those fees to time allocated to projects, and hope there is money left over once the ribbon is cut.[8] Operating margins, typically salted away to cover cash flow challenges and buffer the business from difficult times, are rarely up to this task, and even the highest performing firms with margins above 25% are extraordinary.

Hence the following question: if architects are a relatively rare commodity (which normally drives up prices) and deliver such important service to society (by creating all the buildings that it needs to function) why have we done such a poor job converting the clear value we deliver into an understanding by clients and the public, and, as a desirable consequence, getting paid accordingly?

Compensation propositions

Low margins and salaries are just the symptoms of this larger challenge. The strongest single indicator of the value proposition challenge of our profession are the compensation strategies most often used by architects to get paid for their work. These approaches fall generally into two categories: lump sum or 'fixed' fees; and variable, usually 'by the hour' fees. Generally speaking, the selection of a given compensation model for a project is a function of how well the scope of service is understood by the client and the architect, as the clearer the scope of service, the higher the desire by the client to assign a specific cost of architectural services to the overall project budget. Paying the architect a fixed fee is also the best way for the client to negotiate the lowest price while transferring the financial risk of the architectural fee over to the architects themselves. By paying the architect a fixed amount of money for all the effort required to complete a project, the client is no longer concerned with whether the architect is working efficiently, or, frankly, what the effect of various client demands for extra work might be. Fixed fees also

8 And that a subsequent lawsuit does not further attack the profit margin that remains.

create a reciprocal perverse relationship, dis-incentivizing the architect from working, since less work done means less time spent, less salary paid, and more profit dropping to the bottom line.

Lowest first cost priorities and behaviors

A vast majority of compensation paid to architects in the U.S. and Europe is some variant of a lump sum fee, with only about 15–20% of payments made on an hourly rate basis.[9] Lump sum payments to architects fit into the larger financial culture of the larger building industry, where finding the lowest initial cost for anything — a design fee, a contractor's overhead, material prices, subcontractor bids and so on — is the cardinal rule that drives almost every financial decision on a building project. Maintaining this 'competitive tension' and optimizing the need to assure lowest price, almost at all costs, limits the strategies for architects to increase fees and profitability. In the case of fixed fees, where the architect and team has agreed to provide a (one hopes, well-defined) scope of service to the client for a fixed amount of money, there are only two real ways to increase operating margins. First, and

4.1.3

most important, is obviously to negotiate the highest possible fee at the outset. Given that the fee has likely been set as part of the commoditized procurement approach common to projects (and shopped intensively by the client), this is something of a one-time option that, like any commodity, has limited elasticity. The second, once the fee is set, is to work as efficiently as possible,[10] converting every hour spent into progress toward the completion of the project. Note, however, that neither the underlying platform of the fixed fee itself, nor any strategy to make it more profitable, creates any additional value whatsoever for the client or the project, but are rather optimized by the client for the lowest possible financial cost and risk.

Hourly rate fees

Unfortunately, hourly rate fees do not offer a better option, at least for architects. Under that approach, every hour worked on the project is charged to the client at a pre-set rate, and those rates are a function of the market rather than an indicator of value per se; a firm principal or senior architect can only charge what is normal for similar firms in the same market. And while an hourly fee is elastic — stretching with the amount of work needed — it has built-in profit margin on every hour worked. Lawyers have solved this problem by convincing clients that their hourly time is very valuable (sometimes pushing $1,000 an hour) and unlimited — the best of both worlds

9 Kermit Baker, Jennifer Riskus et al., "AIA Firm Survey Report: The Business of Architecture 2016," p. 18, and Architects Council of Europe, *The Architectural Profession in Europe 2016, a Sector Study* (Architect's Council of Europe, 2017), p. 37.

10 It should be noted, however, that architects are trained in design studio culture where time is immaterial and sleep often optional. While this is an indication of a dedication to the craft, it also creates disrespect for time as a fungible and valuable resource. For evidence that architecture majors work more than their compatriots on campus, see Julia Ingalls, "Architecture Majors Work the Hardest in College, Study Reveals," *Archinet News* (2017), https://archinet.com/news/article/149990764/architecture-majors-work-the-hardest-in-college-study-reveals.

4.1.3 Distribution of fee typologies in the US

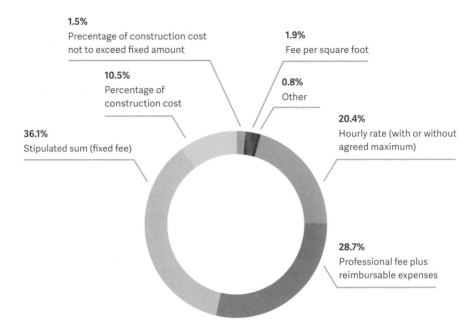

1.5%
Precentage of construction cost not to exceed fixed amount

1.9%
Fee per square foot

10.5%
Percentage of construction cost

0.8%
Other

36.1%
Stipulated sum (fixed fee)

20.4%
Hourly rate (with or without agreed maximum)

28.7%
Professional fee plus reimbursable expenses

that, in the commoditized marketplace of building, would never fly for architects, who work at much lower rates and typically with caps on the maximum fee that can be paid.

Value expressions So architect's compensation models can be seen as tangible expressions of value conversion, where the measurable results — in salaries paid and profits generated — strongly suggest a disconnect between value provided and compensation received. Pressing the mechanics of those models is a limited proposition at best. What are other options?

"Emerging Modes of Architectural Practice" Design strategist Mia Scharphie studied various practices that were experimenting with new models and suggests a framework,[11] based on The Business Model Canvas,[12] for how value might be created. In her study she proposes that value optimization is a function of two categories: internal inputs that generate costs, and external inputs that optimize revenue. The

4.1.4 model is described graphically in Figure 4.1.4 and includes the following variables:

11 Mia Scharphie, *Emerging Modes of Architectural Practice* (Northeastern University School of Architecture, 2015), https://camd.northeastern.edu/architecture/portfolio/emerging-modes-architecture-practice/.
12 Alexander Osterwalder, Yves Pigneur and Tim Clark, *Business Model Generation: A Handbook for Visionaries, Game Changers, and Challengers* (Hoboken, NJ: Wiley, 2010).

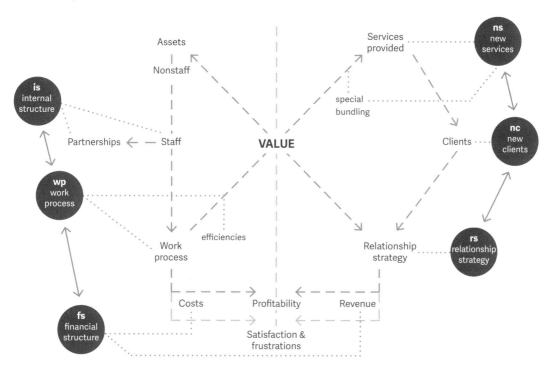

Internal inputs which incur cost:

— **Work process (WP)** how does the firm perform its work, and what is unique about that process or its results?

— **Internal structure (IS)** how does a firm organize its intellectual resources and relationships to key external partners (like engineers)?

— **Financial structure (FS)** how does a firm convert fees to effort, prices services, and run the financial operating model?

External inputs which generate revenue:

— **New clients (NC)** can a firm expand the range of potential targets that can benefit from its services?

— **New services (NS)** can the firm create new offerings or processes that uniquely leverage its skills, talents or willingness to accept risk?

— **Relationship strategy (RS)** can the firm create new connections and exchanges of value with the other parts of the delivery supply chain?

While Scharphie's approach was designed as a classification system by which she could explain the strategies of new practices she examined, it is also an elegant set of strategic levers to consider when trying to redefine new, more effective value propositions. Each variable is an indicator of a potential change to how a practice is run that could create new value, revenue and profits. Choosing one or more of these levers, however, does not in and of itself create new value unless done in the service of a fundamental change in constricted "money for time spent' operating models of today's practice. Once you choose that idea, turning the 'dials' of the Scharphie model can help tune the approach. But how do you choose which dial?

Aligning project objectives for value

One of the most salient features of today's commoditized delivery models for building — and in particular fixed fee contracts for architects — is the utter disconnect between the objectives of a project and the methods the owner uses to procure that project. Architects, acting in their role as agents of the owner, create designs that allegedly embrace the owner's desires for a building, but there's an important trade-off: in exchange for paying that fixed fee described above, the owner cannot specify the actual performative characteristics of the project contractually, given that the architect is fundamentally bound only by the standard of care and standards of professional conduct.[13] It is difficult, if not impossible, to tie the architect's contract and fee to those parameters. All owners want basic performance by their designers and builders: deliver a functioning, technically sufficient, aesthetically appropriate product on time and budget. Sadly, there is a strong chance in today's environment that one or more of these constraints will not be met.[14]

So finding ways to meet these basic requirements — and committing accordingly — is a first value opportunity. Beyond simple cooperation with builders to achieve these ends, architects might actually carefully choose other nodes in the building design network to connect and change, to assure the proper delivery of the building product, leveraging rich design information coming from design (likely to be met by equally provocative information from the builder) and, working together to assure the result, commit to the owner about the outcome. This is a basic principle of the emerging model known as IPD, or integrated project delivery.

The opportunity of outcomes: sketches of the future

But beyond the basics of competent delivery most owners build to accomplish other ends: deliver health care, teach students, sell things. There are compelling metrics associated with each of these objectives: infection rates and patient satisfaction results, test scores, sales per square foot of store area. So commitment to outcomes beyond the basics of competent building, more deeply connected to the real desires and objectives of the project, is

13 Professionals like doctors, lawyers or architects do not promise specific results but rather endeavor to be professionally competent. Further, professional liability insurance specifically disallows coverage for any promises, known in contractual parlance as "warrantees and guaranties."
14 According to McKinsey, 61% of construction projects fail to meet their schedule targets. See McKinsey Global Institute, "Reinventing Construction: A Route to Higher Productivity," p. 30.

perhaps the richest vein of value to be mined by the modern architect. What if the core payments to architects were not an exchange of time for money but rather a reward for accomplishing performative goals of the project? Breaking the tyranny of commoditized fixed fees this way will require the fullest deployment of modern design techniques, combined with a healthy dose of nerve, since doing so works against decades of tradition and conditioning of normal practice.

Scharphie's study identifies twenty-two practices with emerging value propositions that bear further examination. Sketched below are a few possible example value propositions that embrace some of the principles described above, and summarized in Figure 4.1.5.

4.1.5

— **Design information exchange** The architect has prepared detailed models with controlling geometry for the structural frame, including necessary clearances and connection locations. In a side agreement with the steel fabricator, the architect provides the structural geometry in exchange for a fee. The structural engineer and architect work together to confirm the coherence of the geometry and the data. The engineer saves the project time and money and provides the architect with a cash bonus for this work.

— **Cost estimating optimization** A project being delivered by a construction manager (CM) is fast-tracked, with multiple interlocking bid packages for the foundations, site prep, superstructure, enclosure, interior systems, MEP and interior finishes respectively. As the CM is to provide a guaranteed maximum price (GMP) that cannot be exceeded, continuous cost monitoring is needed and there is no time for separate cost estimates in parallel for the various bid packages. Working with design team, the construction manager prepares a data specification with detailed requests for information that is extracted from the building information models created by the architect and her engineers, feeding the continuous cost estimate. This smooths the estimating process, allows more frequent cost iterations. The client has provided a cash incentive to the CM for bringing the project in under the promised GMP. The CM shares this incentive payment with the design team when the project comes in below target.

— **Design-build collaboration** The architect has proposed a complex facade enclosure system for a prominent project. The client is excited about this solution, but wants assurances that the project can meet budget, schedule and energy performance criteria established in the brief. The architect has worked out, as part of the design process, many of the details of fabrication, connection and weather enclosure working closely with a local fabricator. The solution is unique but because of the nature of the design itself and the connection system it can easily be adapted to

Opportunity	Current State	Future State
Design information exchange	Information is transmitted on paper, or via CAD files with a disclaimer saying "use at your own risk."	Designers transfer data directly to the contractor and get paid for its value.
Cost estimation optimization	Cost estimates are derived at specific milestones of the project and slow progress as they are computed and reconciled to budget.	The design team provides the estimation team a continuous flow of information allowing "real time" estimating as the design develops.
Design-build collaboration	The architect works with consultants (and sometimes a fabricator) but hopes for the best result after.	Architects use their understanding of digital fabrication techniques to conjoin with builders to create new systems and products.
Net-zero savings cost sharing	Building performance of the ultimate product is unrelated to the architect's scope of service, contract or fee.	The designers are rewarded if the building reaches net zero by sharing in the cost savings to the owner.
Patient health outcome incentives	Strategic objectives of a building are unrelated to the architect's responsibilities.	Designers predict, design to, and make commitments about what a building 'does' instead of what it 'is.'

other projects. Rather than bid the project out, the architect and fabricator decide to form a new company and deliver the building enclosure as the inaugural project. The subcontract includes delivery time, cost and energy conservation performance incentives to be paid to the successful installer in addition to reasonable profit on the installation itself, divided by the architect and fabricator. They subsequently go on to form a successful company.

— **Net zero energy savings cost sharing** The client hires an architect to design a building which must achieve a LEED certification of Platinum and meet all related requirements. In addition, the client has asked for a project operating at net zero energy, which requires considerable additional investment in both design time and building infrastructure. Achieving LEED certification gets energy consumption well below code requirements, but there is further to go to get to net zero. The client agrees that for every year the building achieves actual net zero in energy usage the architect and contractor will receive a stipend equal to 50% of the cost of the resulting energy savings, without limit. Should the building achieve net positive energy (producing more energy than it consumes) the bonus increases to 60%.

— **Patient health outcome incentives** Under evolving reimbursement models for health care, insurers (including the government) offer strong incentives to reduce the number of hospital-borne infections suffered by patients when under care. Reducing infections is a function of proper maintenance protocols, room configurations, motion of air in patient, treatment and operating rooms and staff procedures. Based on data collected from hundreds of other hospitals, the architects and hospital administration develop a design that, combined with enforceable procedures, should reduce said infections by 40%. The hospital and the architects agree that, assuming that staff follow accepted protocols, every year the hospital achieves reduced infection rates the firm will be paid a performance bonus equal to 20% of the savings captured in higher reimbursements by the insurers.

Each of these ideas extrapolates on the strategy that outcomes, and not commodity, are the real output, deliverable and expectation of architectural design. The first two are easily accomplished by pushing the current boundaries of contracts and scopes of services for architects, which anticipate that the architect is informationally cooperative with the project team and takes some responsibility for cost outputs, but neither is a set goal of a typical project. The latter three press into new territory where the architect is dangerously close to 'making promises' about her services, a risk management taboo that has, in the main, held architects back from delivering value.

Warranty and guarantee

As providers of professional services, architects do not, under typical circumstances, 'warrant' that their performance generates specific results. This is called a 'guarantee' or 'warranty' and professional liability insurance coverage expressly excludes it. The theory here is that, much like doctors or lawyers, architects render their best judgment but cannot absolutely promise specific outcomes. XL Insurance suggests the following:

> By certifying, guaranteeing or warranting something, you are assuming a level of liability well beyond the legally required standard of care. Your professional liability insurance is not intended to cover breach of contract or warranty, the assumption of someone else's liability or a promise to perform to a standard of care higher than legally required. The smallest error, whether caused by you or someone else, could lead to a claim of breach of warranty.[15]

It is highly unlikely that architects will ever escape the bounds of commodification if we are not willing to challenge these traditions and constraints.

---

15 See http://xlcatlin.com/fast-fast-forward/articles/top-10-contract-clauses-for-design-professionals.

4.2

Producing Design Process

If different value propositions are to be found, how does this change the work process, relationships and artifacts of practice?

The various scenarios described at the end of the previous chapter suggest emergent strategies for new value generation by architects, based on the premise that the real value of architectural design is to make things happen, rather than produce drawings for builders and shield clients from risk. The productive, predictive and analytical capabilities of technology, combined with architects' innate ability to wrestle 'wicked' problems to the ground, make this new value proposition possible. The value conversion mechanism that connects this idea to the systems of delivery is outcome-based compensation and project execution models where the architect has a different role, responsibilities, assumptions of risk and rewards. These are hardly small adjustments to current practice, but rather seismic shifts in how services are provided, deliverables generated and distributed and professional standards of competence measured.

New service models through flexible specialization

Labor economist Paolo Tombesi has suggested that architects have traditionally considered 'design services' as too narrowly focused on the formulation, massing, function and expression of a building, and new value approaches certainly will require breaking from those particular barriers. He posits that the making of a building is comprised of a larger collection of related design services that articulate a wide range of necessary steps and outcomes, and proposed one such construct in an essay written in 2006 and

4.2.1   diagrammed in Figure 4.2.1.[16] Tombesi recommends that 'building design' itself require five coordinated area of activity, each generated by a series of related tasks. His intent was not so much to redefine the traditional building design process, or even the standard taxonomy of the architect's scope of service (see Chapter 3.2, "Information Coherence") memorialized as the phases of 'predesign,' 'schematic design' and so forth, but rather to recom-

16 Tombesi, "On the Cultural Separation of Labor."

mend that the architect's design responsibilities are much more widely applicable across the delivery cycle of design and construction. Not only are architects capable of doing everything in this network, but their businesses should adapt a concept he calls "flexible specialization" — the ability to transfer the core competency of design throughout this network and apply those skills wherever needed. This has the dual benefit of creating a greater range of services that the architect can sell as well as extending the value proposition of the architect's participation in the core activities of building. The architect should build more capable 'design muscles' across the supply chain and move into different parts of the network depending on demand and economic conditions, a strategy that will be absolutely necessary to flip the model of commoditized services.

Flexible specialization combines all three of Scharphie's external levers (new clients, services and sources of revenue, see Chapter 4.1, "Creating Value Through Design") by suggesting that designers can ply their trade doing new things to support delivery. As a consequence, they build new rela-

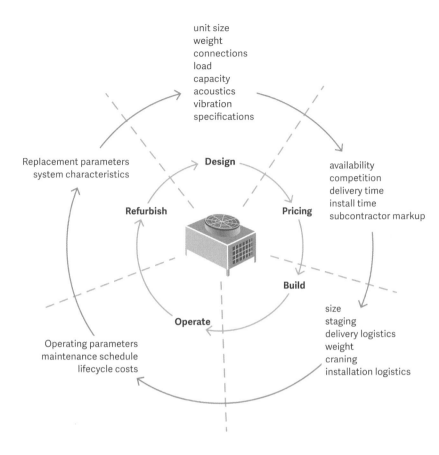

unit size
weight
connections
load
capacity
acoustics
vibration
specifications

Replacement parameters
system characteristics

Design

availability
competition
delivery time
install time
subcontractor markup

Refurbish

Pricing

Build

Operate

size
staging
delivery logistics
weight
craning
installation logistics

Operating parameters
maintenance schedule
lifecycle costs

tionships across that supply chain and provide greater value to both current, traditional clients as well as new ones: the recipients of the design deliverables in new realms like building production or even building use and maintenance. It is hard to argue that there are no opportunities for the architect to take renewed interest in how buildings are formulated, produced, erected and used, particularly in an era where those processes either originate in or depend upon the digital design information that the architect creates as part of her core services.

4.2.2

Recalibrating risk and reward

This strategic recommendation —"design more of the building and the processes that produce it" — seems obvious. If design skill is the common denominator across the building design process, why haven't architects exploited this opportunity to create value? The central challenge is a question of defining that value, and in this case, its relationship to risk and reward. Others have written at great length about the diminution of the architect's responsibilities and role in the building process and our inability to face and

4.2.3 CAD versus BIM coordination of a given element

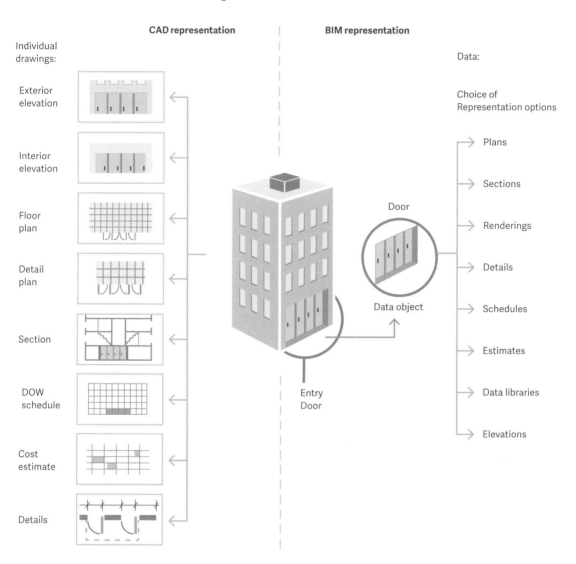

CAD representation

Individual drawings:

Exterior elevation

Interior elevation

Floor plan

Detail plan

Section

DOW schedule

Cost estimate

Details

BIM representation

Data:

Door

Choice of Representation options

→ Plans

→ Sections

→ Renderings

→ Details

→ Schedules

→ Estimates

→ Data libraries

→ Elevations

Data object

Entry Door

embrace some of the inherent risks of the building process.[17] But a well-known dynamic of any marketplace is the relationship between risk and reward, where assumption and control of the former yields the latter. The liability crisis of the 1980s reified the presumption by professional liability carriers that architects were unable to manage risk (see Chapter 4.4, "New Value in the Systems of Delivery"), and thereby should attempt to divest themselves of as much risk as possible (and thereby protect their insurance companies

17 For a particularly poignant view of this question, see Atkins and Simpson, *Managing Project Risk: Best Practices for Architects and Related Professionals.*

from exposure). The resulting attitude created a generation of practitioners who instinctively partitioned themselves from any activity — cost estimating, schedule design, remediation — that might increase their liability exposure. This ingrained attitude has not served the profession well in the decades since, as the industry has grown more complex, challenging and risky. We may have avoided the risks, but have missed enormous opportunities to better serve clients, deliver value and enhance profits.

The wide availability of advanced digital tools that make the work of the architect more reliable, accurate, predictable and efficient challenges the architect's now instinctual avoidance of risk. A first example: hand or CAD-generated drawings, no longer really up to the task of describing today's complex buildings, are giving way to BIM-generated projects where information is integrated and coordinated both graphically and physically. Badly coordinated drawings, where a given building element drafted in different places in a working drawing set might contain inconsistencies and errors creating liability, are far less likely to happen when those same drawings are reports from a BIM database. Elements in that database are digitally coordinated in three-dimensional space, allowing interferences and other integration issues to be resolved during design rather than in the field. A single set of doors must be drawn multiple times in different views in CAD, while all of its representations can be extracted as "data reports" from a BIM model, as
4.2.3   described in Figure 4.2.3.

Performance characteristics of the building, from simple issues like shadows and daylighting to more complex questions of building energy performance, can be predicted *a priori* by analytical and simulation software. Design solutions can be more systematically generated and explored by a combination of generative design via scripts bound to evaluation by this analysis software. In total, design methodology is more precise, complete and accurate than ever before, and fit for purpose for today's complex building problems. Given that more reliable technical behavior and performance of a building should result, why not commit to such outcomes as a fundamental value of architectural services?

At this juncture, practitioners reading this text are starting to feel a bit queasy. Overcoming the emotional and financial barriers to this strategy — assuming more responsibility in exchange for more control and reward — is to run in a direction completely opposite from what the profession has done for the last forty years. The exchange of design services for fees based on time — rather than results — provides a certain sense of relief for architects who can always allege that 'doing one's best' in the service of the project, and thereby (barely) meeting the standard of care, is a defense for an allegation of negligence. And since architects do not 'make things' but 'provide judgment' then this idea veers dangerously close to a product liability standard. Queasiness, indeed.

CESAR PELLI & ASSOCIATES

☐ REVIEWED

☐ REVIEWED AS NOTED

☐ REVISE AND RESUBMIT

☐ REVIEW NOT APPLICABLE

REVIEW BY CESAR PELLI & ASSOCIATES CONSTITUTES REVIEW OF THE AESTHETIC DESIGN INTENTIONS OF THIS MATERIAL ONLY. CESAR PELLI & ASSOCIATES ASSUMES NO RESPONSIBILITY FOR TECHNICAL, LEGAL OR CONSTRUCTION MATTERS NOR DO THEY ASSUME RESPONSIBILITY FOR DIMENSIONAL ACCURACY AND COORDINATION.

PROJECT _____

REVIEWED BY _____

DATE _____ XXX _____

The author prepared this exculpatory text that accompanied any CAD data transmitted to his firm's collaborators, designed to protect the firm from unanticipated uses of that data.

Redefining deliverables

The contractual term for "the stuff the architect produces through her work" is "instruments of service," a phrase specifically designed to indicate that drawings, models, digital data and all such materials are a means to an end, and not an end in and of themselves. The distinction originates from another important idea that the things that the architect creates are not products[18] — which are held to a different liability standard like appliances or cars — but rather merely the vessels in which the architect's ideas are held as the architect provides her services and they move around the delivery system. Those ideas should always be transmitted "accompanied" by the architect's supervision and judgment, since that is what the client is ultimately paying for and the standard by which the competence of the architect is measured.

As architects turned from producing drawings manually to 'electrifying' drafting using CAD, an interesting set of questions emerged about the resulting digital data. Once committed to paper, either approach created an abstraction of the proposed design, projected in plan, section and elevation

---

18 This is an important contrast, because products are held to a different, and more strict, performance standard than are services, but the associated liability can be assigned to a company. Design liability is always borne by the individual architect.

on the page and heavily annotated with dimensions, cross-references and annotated notes. Hand drafting occurred at the scale of drawing as the entire building was translated from its full-scale, intended dimensions to a fractional size (like 1/8" = 1'-0" or 1:500) in the mind's eye of the drafter. But the geometry of CAD was created in digital 'space' at full scale and then simply plotted on the paper at the abstracted scale, making a 'full scale' version of the building's geometry easily accessible to designers, collaborators, builders and fabricators, who could use that data to create shop drawings, construction strategies and integration plans of the overall build.

But alas, not so fast. Citing concerns about unexpected use of that data, or even unanticipated errors buried deep in the digital description, most firms would allow users to "rely only on the plotted drawing" as an instrument of service, hardly an opportunity to leverage additional value of the better information. Worse, when contractors demanded this data of the architects and engineers — channeling the desires of their builders — firms often just handed it over without even a whimper or a request to be paid for it. In a world replete with digital and analytical models, we are not going back to analog construction and it is best if architects decide that their design data has convertible value not only to builders, but to owners operating their buildings.

4.2.4

A transactional
decision

In any traditional delivery model (like Design Bid Build, for example) this is a transactional decision: the data has specific monetary value to users downstream, and architects should simply sell it to those requesters with a value commensurate to the time saved by the receiving party, plus further consideration for the potential risks of misinterpretation or misuse. The mistake, often made, is to fail to anticipate the value of digital design data when negotiating contract terms, and then caving to subsequent demands. If the terms of such an exchange are not negotiated as part of the architect's agreement for services, the opportunity is lost.

In future outcome-based models, however, deliverables return to their original means-to-an-end purpose beyond mere competency, but now correlated to the defined outcomes of the project and exchanged freely between the project players who might require them. As the overall design-to-construction process is digitized across a spectrum of tasks and processes, the architect's deliverables will be measured by a new standard with two distinct characteristics. First, are they sufficiently integrated into the overall constellation of the project, relating to and amplifying other deliverables created by the project team, and do they accurately reflect the progress of design development and 'work' with adjacent data? And then second, do they progress the project in a demonstrable way toward the agreed-upon outcomes defined at the outset?

As architects become more adept with predictive tools, their ability to assert outcomes will be more assured, and one hopes continually expand to more important and valuable implications of the design-build-operate

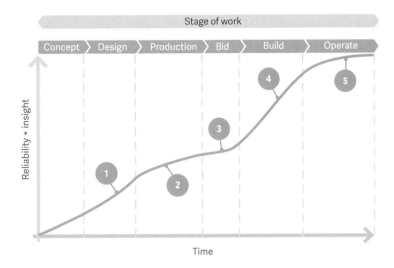

Information Reliability: As a project progresses in digital form, understanding and insight increase with each stage of the work, and a BIM-based process offers immediate benefits in the reliability of the resulting data:

1 — During early design, digital models provide three-dimensional clarity and transparency for the clients, designers and builders, particularly to those who can't read plans or elevations. Early quantity take-offs are derived from the models rather than measured from drawings.

2 — During production of technical documentation for construction, model-based production is inherently coordinated, reducing errors where traditional drawings often contain mismatches of representations or information.

3 — During the bidding process, builders can understand and query characteristics of the "virtual building" rather than rely exclusively on paper documents.

4 — During construction, the builders can virtually simulate construction approach and sequencing to optimize the approach.

5 — As the building is running, data derived from the models created in previous stages can assist the operators in understanding performance criteria, maintenance information, as well as more easily located physical assets in the structure.

4.2.5   process. One such progression might look like Figure 4.2.5: The diagram suggests that, as time progresses from left to right, precision and prediction will expand the service and deliverable opportunities that are the natural artifacts of design process, and value can be converted accordingly.

Exchanges of value in new relationships and delivery

Traditional instruments of service are artifacts of the relationships between clients, designers and builders, operating in contexts established by delivery models and associated contracts and circumscribed by performance standards and transactions, all of which are likely to be overturned by the outcome-based potential of technology-enabled design and construction.

Integrated project delivery (IPD)

There is strong early evidence for this proposition in the emergence of integrated project delivery (IPD) in the United States, a model where collaboration between the players is strongly privileged, agreed-upon outcomes rewarded by extra profit, and liability stemmed by promises of the delivery team not to sue each other. Interestingly, the concept of IPD emerged simultaneously in the US with that of BIM, with the presumption that the technology would provide enough transparent collaboration between the parties that new ways of delivering projects became possible.

The heart of the IPD value proposition is at direct odds, however, with traditional delivery models, to wit: all players in the process are aligned behind objectives that operate in the interest of the project and that are co-incident with their own. For example, if it has been determined by the owner/architect/builder team that meeting a schedule is critically important, then the team is paid a portion of its profit to accomplish this goal, under the presumption that modern, IPD-based collaboration methods reliant on digital technology make accomplishing that goal possible. The transformation of fundamental relationships, catalyzed by tools, is perhaps the most profound change that architects can expect as outcome-based models emerge, and emblematic of the decommoditization of design contracts that this book endorses.

Shifting professional standards

Implied here are parallel developments in scopes of services, structure of deliverables, relationships between the delivery partners and business models of delivery. These developments are underpinned by what is likely an even more important transformation in the competency standard. The Standard Standard of Care (SOC) of Care (SOC) (see also Chapter 2.4, "Preparing Digital Designers") is a term of contractual art that refers to an otherwise undefined indicator of what is competent, non-negligent performance by the architect, roughly measured as "what another competent architect would have done in similar circumstances." The SOC is not written down somewhere as a matter of law, but rather is the basis of an argument about whether, usually in the circumstance where someone has asserted a claim of negligence against the architect, that architect failed to measure up against our common understanding of what good practice might be (see Chapter 2.3, "The Evolution of Responsible Control and Professional Care").

Since the SOC is, by definition, backward-looking,[19] it moves with the 'invisible hand' of the marketplace, and technology's future effect is unpredictable. In the early 2000s, when BIM began to emerge as a new technology, there was plenty of hand wringing — particularly by the insurance and legal industries — about potential pitfalls and dangers that might outweigh its benefits in precision and accuracy. A typical warning read like this:

19 Dan Bradshaw, "The Rewards and Risks of BIM," *Benchmark Review* 6 (2006), http://www.benchmark-insurance.com/BIM.pdf.

BIM changes the dynamics between you and your clients. Project owner expectations can sour and need to be carefully managed. Your clients may anticipate faster, error-free and therefore lower-cost projects. They need to be educated that BIM will likely result in higher design fees to reflect your increased scope of services and levels of responsibility in managing project information... because you are managing the compilation of and access to project information from multiple sources, lines of responsibility are blurred. There are not unified standards for how BIM projects are managed and who is responsible for what. Your initial ventures with BIM are especially fraught with danger. You can expect missteps, redundancies, and gaps in performance until parties become experienced and comfortable with the new design process.[20]

This is what my mom used to call "'damning by faint praise," where benefits have been transformed into potential pitfalls. A future of "error-free" and "lower-cost" buildings hardly sounds dangerous, and the eventual benefits of an empowered project team are likely to stretch well beyond those modest goals. Ironically, the only BIM-related case law currently on the books asserted that the architect was negligent for failing to use BIM on a badly coordinated project.[21]

The SOC as a measure of professional competence will likely remain even as the architect's participation in a building is required and remunerated, but the definition of competence itself will shift. Competent practice will be measured in the putative gap between the described originating outcomes of a project (defined collaboratively between the players at the outset of work), the architect's ability to work in integrated fashion toward those ends during project development, and her specific, identifiable failures to protect the public health, safety and welfare as may be defined at the time. All justifiably moving targets that should shift in response to new delivery models and the architect's role within them.

20 Ibid.
21 Leslie P. Holmes and Karen King, "Evolving Practice and the Standard of Care: Sustainability, Security and Everything in Between," *Proceedings of the 54th Annual Meeting of Invited Attorneys — Victor O Schinnerer* (2015), p. 112.

4.3

Calibrating
Design Values

How is value measured and success defined in digital practice?

'Value' is an economic term, a way of measuring what something might be worth often in terms of something else. The measurement of value is a function of either an independent parameter (like a currency) or whatever metric the exchanging parties are willing to agree upon. In the building industry, of which architecture is a main constituent, value exchange may involve payment, transfer of risk, allocation of materials and/or labor, or information. These flows create a network of exchanges between a project's client, designers, and builders, but by implication also affect the users, financiers, regulators, and public itself.

Measuring value in the building industry

It is the combination of these flows that creates the overall result of the delivery process, the 'valued' result that the client is looking for: a building. By definition, every player in the process either delivers or receives a payment in exchange for receiving or providing value of some sort; the architect is paid by the client, and subsequently pays her consultants for their work. A bank sends funds to the client by loaning it money for construction until another bank provides a mortgage. The contractor receives payment from the client to cover overhead, profit margin, and costs caused by resources like material suppliers and subcontractors.

But moving the project forward requires more and other kinds of exchanges. The builder's primary exchange is the conversion of the value of materials and labor that manifests as construction for that money, while the architect's is her judgment as represented by the information communicated in the instruments of service. Implicit in the various business deals between all the players, described in Figure 4.3.1, are payments in consideration of the assumed risks of the work.

4.3.1

There can be other measures. While economic theory tends to convert value exclusively to money, so-called Triple Bottom Line economics (or TBL) suggests that value cannot be exclusively convertible to currency since the implications of a transaction are widespread. TBL frames value exchange in a number of dimensions: social (value to people), environmental (value to

4.3.1 AEC value exchanges

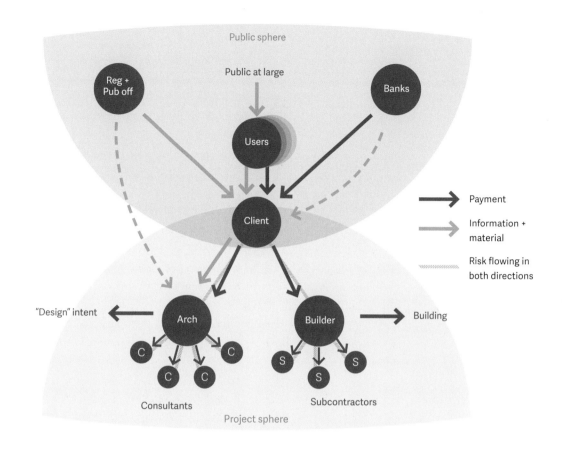

Public sphere

Reg + Pub off

Public at large

Banks

Users

Client

→ Payment

→ Information + material

Risk flowing in both directions

"Design" intent ← Arch

Builder → Building

C C C C

Consultants

S S S

Subcontractors

Project sphere

4.3.2 Values hierachy

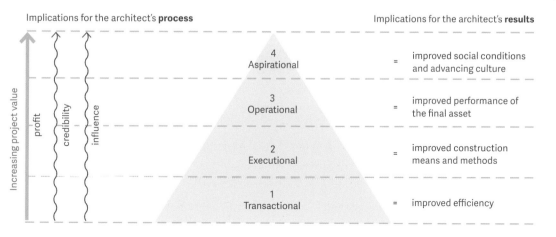

Implications for the architect's **process**

Implications for the architect's **results**

Increasing project value

profit | credibility | influence

4 Aspirational = improved social conditions and advancing culture

3 Operational = improved performance of the final asset

2 Executional = improved construction means and methods

1 Transactional = improved efficiency

the planet), and financial (value of profit), thereby considering ramifications that are not so easily monetized. TBL suggests that value propositions for the built environment are not exclusively reduced to financial gain.

Addressed elsewhere in this text (see Chapter 4.1, "Creating Value Through Design") is the well-trodden trope that architects do not make money and seemingly do not care much about business. I have argued elsewhere[22] that, in those terms, there is a strong disconnect between the contribution made by architects to the building process and environment and how we are compensated. And since value is primarily an economic consideration, a 'value hierarchy' can guide an understanding of what improved value and related success may look like for a technologically empowered profession, sketched in Figure 4.3.2.

4.3.2

Proposed here is a progression of value generation ideas, based on the notion that technology provides the architect with a more reliable, precise, and predictive toolkit from which to generate, test, elaborate, and collaborate her design concepts, from which there are immediate value opportunities to generate profit, credibility, and project control. The assumption underlying this vision of a progression is that the architect's successful delivery of results within this hierarchy should be compensated accordingly. While the mechanisms for such compensation are examined further in the next chapter, let us here look at the three main value opportunities involved.

Transactional value Architects are commonly accused of 'never stopping the design,' an aphorism about three converging sensibilities: first, the project moves from conceptual abstraction to finished physical asset without every possible decision being made at a level of detail necessary for construction; second, the design process is iterative as conditions and understanding of constraints evolve over time and require a response irrespective of the moment in the project timeline at which they occur; and finally, under typical fixed-fee arrangements and tight schedules, the architect rarely has sufficient time and money to complete every dimension of the design before handing it over to the builder.[23] The challenge presented by this approach is obvious: how do the architect's collaborators know when something is 'finished' so that they can rely upon information provided by the architect? How do they know it is not going to change before they are able to act upon it? Figure 4.3.3 overlays the increasing resolution of project information as the timeline progresses

4.3.3

---

22 See Chapter 2.2, "Defining Design Intent: Depiction, Precision and Generation," and Phillip G. Bernstein, "Money, Value, Architects, Building," *Perspecta* 47, "Money" (2014).

23 In fact, it is generally understood that different competent architects, working on the same project, will likely produce different sets of construction contract documents to give to the builder. While the documents would have the same general organization and structure, they would differ according to individual experience and choices about level of detailing and other particulars. Thus, there is no such thing as a "standard, complete" set of technical documents, at least under today's standard of care. These differences are sometimes exploited by builders who accuse architects of failing to complete documents to sufficient levels of resolution for them to bid and build projects.

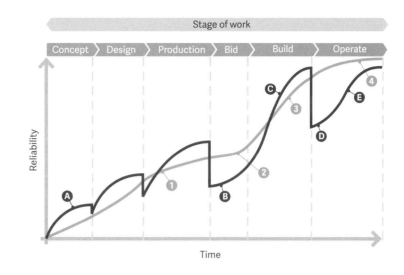

As a project progresses and its design is further refined, in theory the resolution of information about the project should be of increasing accuracy and resolution, as described in the green line in the chart above:

1 — The design team progressively develops the project until "design intent" is defined.

2 — Once the design is passed to the builder to bid and construct, information resolution accelerates as detailed decisions about materials and construction are made.

3 — By the end of the project it exists in physical form along with all the additional information assembled from material purchases, warrantees, etc.

4 — As the building is operated, the owner gains further insight about how it works.

But ironically, as that information passes from phase to phase in the project and is handed over to different teams via drawings, the reliability of that information drops across phase boundaries:

A — Insight climbs as each phase is completed, but a "reset" occurs at the beginning of a subsequent phase as scale increases, level of detail must be adjusted, and new members are added to the team. If the information is communicated only on paper this drop can be dramatic.

B — The biggest drop in fidelity occurs when the design team passes the project to the builder, who has to "figure out" design intent and fill in all the gaps in the construction documents.

C — As the project is built, information accumulates and knowledge about the job advances, but...

D — Once the completed project is handed over to the owner to operate, understanding drops to a new low as the new building and its "instructions" are figured out, slowly, by its new stewards.

relative to the fidelity of information as it is passed along successive project stages.

The conditions of transactional information exchange are changing as schedules shorten and construction becomes more complex, as de-

4.3.4   scribed further in Figure 4.3.4. Where once design progressed as an orderly 'waterfall' of well-understood phases (schematic design, design development, and so forth), today boundaries between project phases are blurry at best, and elements of the design may be explored out to almost fabrication-level of detail in order to test and select a given system. Many projects

4.3.4 Evolution of design and construction phasing

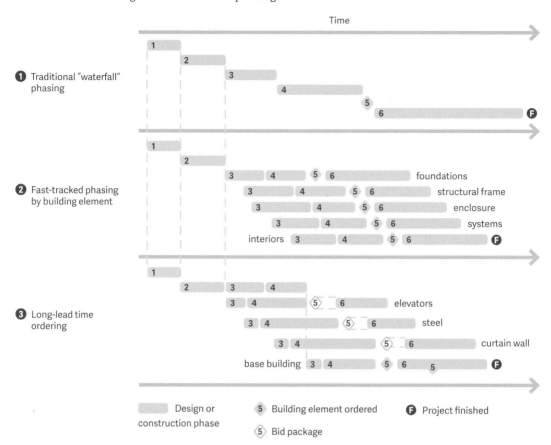

Three sequences of design and construction have evolved as schedules have accelerated and building itself become more complex:

❶ Traditional "waterfall" phasing — where each design and construction phase follows linearly;

❷ Fast-tracked phasing by building element — where after initial design each individual component of the overall building (for example, foundations, structural frame, etc.) is then designed in detail, procured and then built, and

❸ Long-lead time ordering — where the overall arrangement of the construction process is driven by specific items that might require very long manufacturing or delivery times before they're ready to be installed on the project, such as elevators or even steel or curtain wall components during times when construction demand is high.

KEY to PHASING ELEMENTS:

1 — CONCEPT: creating the initial strategy for the design (pre-design)

2 — DESIGN: developing the overall approach and character (schematic design)

3 — TECHNICAL DESIGN: integrating systems and performance (design development)

4 — PRODUCTION DESIGN: preparing documents for procurement and construction (construction documents)

5 — PROCUREMENT: obtaining bids and determining the builder (bid)

6 — CONSTRUCTION: building the project

4.3.5 BIM epistemology

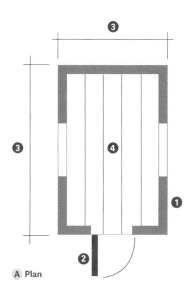

A Plan

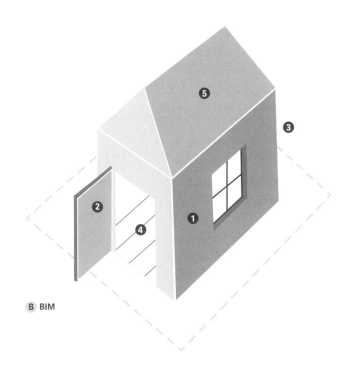

B BIM

Traditional architectural graphics like the floor plan **(A)** imply, but do not specifically articulate, information about building in the same way that a Building Information Model **(B)** may do. While almost all the elements are expressed (except the roof in the floor plan) a BIM instantiates several kinds of knowledge in its representation missing from a graphical plan, including:

— RELATIONSHIPS: Where and how do the walls **(1)** connect to the door **(2)** and floor **(4)**, as well as the roof **(5)**, and how does a window fit into a wall? The rules for such relationships are part of a BIM representation.

— DIMENSIONS: While the overall dimensions in the ground plane are declared in a floor plan **(3)**, their relationships in three dimensions, confirmed by their inherent connections, are all declared in the BIM.

— MATERIALITY: While the makeup of all the elements of the building may be declared by text in **(A)**, BIM data includes this information explicitly.

— PERFORMANCE: With the three-dimensional precision, materiality and relationships explicit in BIM, analytics can predict performance.

are built using the 'fast track' method where, for example, the foundations may well be under construction while the superstructure is completing design and pieces of the design itself are progressively completed, procured, and then constructed. The approach depends upon the reliable succession of design-to-construct decisions, without the benefit of seeing the entire design as a completed integrated whole. Sometimes it is necessary to resolve a given component of the design (like a complex piece of equipment, such as a large air handler) very early in order for it to be delivered to the job site in time for proper installation. This disaggregates the project sequencing even further.

In all cases, the development of the design is progressive and iterative. The insights and precision that model-based design supported by computation analysis and big data collaboration platforms provide will not and should not change that fundamental characteristic. But, particularly in the case of BIM-based design, the reliability of the information platform from which the team is working is substantially increased via the framework that underpins BIM — a consistent epistemological structure where elements have defined characteristics and interrelationships. The level of resolution of each of those elements is explicit in its definition within the BIM, so the players involved understand, when interacting with the emergent design, whether the designer has chosen a specific configuration and resolution, for example, the location and material make-up of a given wall. This procedure leads to a transparent information exchange that is more efficient because everyone understands it. Finally, describing the design as it progresses in model form conveys to the entire design-and-build team a clear view of the current status of design development and clear reference points from which to continue elaboration, ask questions, or build. At the lowest level of value exchange — information about exactly what is happening — precision and reliability have dramatically increased.

4.3.5

A fundamental legal principle of American construction is known as the Spearin Doctrine, which states that the builder of a project is entitled to rely on the accuracy and completeness of the information provided by the client while preparing bids and constructing an asset. That information is provided by the owner's architect, and the question of accuracy and completeness is at the heart of most disputes in construction about whether the drawings were sufficiently complete to commence construction reliably. There is tremendous value created by clarity and precision of model-based digital information that reduces ambiguity and speeds decision making and reliable access, five specific examples of which are outlined in Figure 4.3.6.

Spearin Doctrine

4.3.6

These transactional efficiencies — and related monetary gains — are convertible by the architect in a variety of ways: productivity within the design process yields extra margins; geometry and other metadata in the models can be leveraged by the builders, directly saving them time and money (some of which should revert to the architect); repeated generation of usable data increases the architect's credibility to supply insight across the delivery spectrum; and the direct transfer of such information across the design-build spectrum augments the architect's control over the resulting built artifact. These strategies are just a beginning of what could be a longer-term value proposition for architects to leverage data across the supply chain of building.

Executional value

I have previously examined and explained the architect's obligations — or utter lack thereof — for the contractor's means and methods of construction as the unfortunate result of the convergence of a specific arrangement of convenience at the turn of the twentieth century with the liability crisis at its close (see Chapter 3.3, "Designing Design: Optimizing, Solving, Selecting"). I have further suggested that the ability to memorialize not just the description of the final, built artifact but also the process by which that artifact was constructed will become a regular part of preconceiving a building through a model-based design process to construction combined with the storage and processing capabilities of the cloud. Somewhere in the heady mixture of architectural, engineering, and construction insight that is the building design prior to build, the underlying logics of the construction process will be digitally represented, allowing the team to generate, test, and select optimum solutions based not just on building performance but optimally efficient construction methodology, thereby creating a virtuous cycle of knowledge about how things are made and how they are designed. The information necessary to make this happen will need to flow reciprocally between the designer and constructor, in a process where the former is assuring that build logic supports her design intent, and the latter that the design can be executed. The resulting exchange and related insights thus have what is called here 'executional' value in the delivery of the project, moving beyond the mere 'what needs to be built' toward 'how it gets done,' with each side of the executional equation informing the other.

We are a full step advanced from first-level, transactional information here, because not only is executional information a novel concept for the delivery system, it is a new value proposition as well. Architects can only convert that value by making (and implementing) a two-part case in their contracts. In a first step, executional data will be more work to create, deploy, and manage for the architect during design, which has a cost that should be reimbursed. And in a second step, that same data is a direct line into McKinsey's $1.6 trillion productivity opportunity and the architect deserves a reasonable share of the contractor's (and owner's) efficiency jump. There is a third and toughest side to this, however: the increased risk borne by the architect where her data, in direct use by the builder, connects her work directly to the risks of construction-site failure. The economics of risk-reward should apply here financially as well, particularly when construction goes smoothly across the constraints of safety, schedule, and budget.

Operational value An equally provocative — and potentially potent — opportunity to convert value can be found in the use of buildings that architects design, the 'operational value' exchange shown in item 5 at Figure 4.2.5. Buildings are the frame for a lot of important stuff that happens in everyday life, and that is why owners actually hire architects earlier in the first place — to educate in schools, heal in hospitals, sell things in stores. And architects believe they can make such things happen while selling their services as a commodity — with no obligation for those promises. Why not connect the two ideas? Today it is easy to argue that there are many influences on, say, the design of an elementary school and an increase in standardized test scores, including the abilities of the students and teachers and other environmental factors beyond the direct control of the architect. Over time, however, big data compilations coupled with analysis will make such connections more direct and the ability to model and simulate the behavior of buildings and their occupants more reliable, giving architects a great, if terrifying, new value proposition: being paid to actually make things happen, not just speculating about them.

Some muscle-building can happen with more basic operational commitments in the areas of sustainable building performance (did the building save the energy alleged?), acoustic comfort (did the concert hall meet the expectations of the musicians?) or even maintenance costs (was it as easy to take care of as declared?). Since the operation of a building is said to require between ten and one hundred times its construction cost[24] there are strong incentives for the owner to transfer some of the risk (and the related return) of those obligations to another party — like the architect — who is in a position to study, define, simulate, and properly design an operationally effective solution — and get paid for the result.

Aspirational value Of course, every building has value beyond the financial, despite the industry's relentless desire for lowest first cost. There are proximate parameters of construction — schedule, safety, costs, energy conservation — that are relatively easy to model, analyze, measure, and therefore optimize, but to leave design out of that equation was to permanently endanger it.

Design quality, therefore, is a value of the architectural enterprise that, while difficult to predict, analyze, or measure, must be included in the value proposition of architecture, particularly in a technology-powered design era of the kind predicted here. Anyone who has endured architecture school knows that architects believe that design quality is something that can be understood, discussed, even measured in a non-quantitative way. Questions of social justice or global environmental impact may be measured by the organizations that hire architects to build to answer them, and measures of their success may not convert so directly as the other categories outlined here. Some early IPD projects have defined aspirational values as desired outcomes of their projects and chosen to measure same with mechanisms like surveys (of, say, employee satisfaction) or inspectors (in the case of design quality). In any case, it will be important for architects to make sure that the ineffable aspects of design value generation are not left behind in the quantified and rational wave that design technology will surely bring. But if architects can build the credibility that comes with promises made about

24 See https://www.wbdg.org/resources/life-cycle-cost-analysis-lcca.

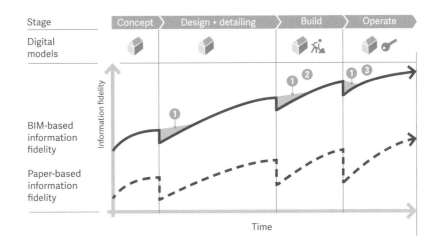

1 — TRANSACTIONAL VALUE: Even though there are likely four different types of digital models of the project along the stage continuum of concept through operation, they easily transition from one stage to the next, making information flow more efficient and less repetitive.

2 — EXECUTIONAL VALUE: During construction, model-based information is more efficient for quantity take-off, coordination, work package design and construction sequencing.

3 — OPERATIONAL VALUE: Model-based information that is derived from design and construction stage models is more fluid, accessible and understandable for the building's operators and occupants.

the rationale, they will be able to extend their influence and control to the ineffable as well.

Value generation opportunities

Thus value generation opportunities exist for the architect across the spectrum of the delivery and operation of a project, bolstered by the precision, accuracy, transparency, and predictive nature of emerging technologies like BIM, simulation, and analysis. Those technologies will be further enhanced in the second digital turn of cloud computation, big data, and machine learning. Figure 4.3.6 attempts to summarize these possibilities, by describing the progression of project stages relative to the fidelity of digital versus non-digital processes. The diagram, organized by project stages, describes the types of digital models required for each stage of a project; it describes the degrees of information fidelity available as each project phase is completed for two cases: in a typical paper-based project (the bottom curve) and a smoother, less ragged information flow enabled by BIM and other technologies (the upper curve). Each vertical drop in these curves represents informational discontinuity in the handoffs between the phases, which is lessened by the informational precision of BIM but on the other hand is also a proxy for a value generation opportunity for the architect.

4.3.7   The matrix outlined in Figure 4.3.7 summarizes the value typologies suggested in this chapter; it provides an example of each and defines how the resulting value might be measured and converted.

Generating value   At the center of the argument for a refined value proposition for architecture is a fundamental belief that architects and architecture are not sufficiently valued by the economic and social systems within which they function. Architects have a wide variety of motivations to work, many of which are not connected to the direct economic benefits of practice. But all indicators — salaries, profitability, market influence — suggest that architecture is largely caught up in the hyper-commoditized procurement models that characterize the overall building delivery system. Technology can offer architects the opportunity to both generate value along the lines described above and convert it to profits should they so choose. Given the inherent inefficiencies built into that commoditized system, it is likely that someone in the supply chain will chase the resulting economic opportunity. Why not architects, whose creativity is at the headwater of the entire enterprise itself?

Value Opportunity	Description	Conversion example	Value example
Transactional	There are reliable point-to-point exchanges of usable design information between players in the delivery chain	The architect provides the lighting fixture installer with precise geometric coordinates of every necessary ceiling and fixture location, saving the installer 400 hours of shop drawing and field coordination time worth $40,000.	The architect charges the subcontractor $15,000 for this information extracted from the BIM, providing XYZ coordinates.
Executional	The design representation uses a combination of geometry, metadata (descriptions) and logic to define a building component.	Working with the curtainwall contractor, the architect defines the precise installation sequence for craning, attaching and sealing the components of the curtainwall system, assuring that it can be accomplished within the aggressive construction schedule and saving 18 full days of construction. General conditions for each day of the build are $20,000 for a project savings of $360,000.	The architect receives a $10,000 fee for incorporating the additional information into the construction documents model. When the time savings are realized, she is paid an additional performance bonus of $36,000. The balance of the savings are distributed to the owner, CM and curtainwall sub.
Operational	The architect agrees to tie her compensation to a specific, measurable improvement in operations based on the use of the project.	The Owner-Architect agreement for the design of a hospital includes a performance requirement for the design that airborne surgical infections are to be reduced by 30% over the first two years of the project. Based on computational fluid dynamic simulations of the operating theaters, the architects create a new configuration that shifts laminar air flow over the surgical field that prevents contaminants from blowing from instruments and the surgical team into the patient wound. Infections drop from 1 per 100 procedures to 1 per 500, saving $1.5 million a year in additional costs.	After confirming that the operating theaters have been built, commissioned and staffed correctly, the owner begins the two-year incentive period and realizes $3.75 million in post-surgical savings due to dramatic reductions in infection rates. The architects are paid a $350,000 bonus in two installments over the incentive period.
Aspirational	The project aims to achieve responsible social equity goals during its overall lifetime.	The architect works with a local NGO that provides an array of services including housing and health care to the homeless in an urban community beset with that challenge. She designs a pre-fabricated, ready-to-build solution that can be repeated as the NGO raises capital.	The NGO builds twice as many units as originally planned and reduced homelessness in the city by 20% the first year. The architect becomes a nationally recognized designer of such housing and attracts new design talent from across the globe.

4.4

New Values in the Systems of Delivery

How is the agency of the architect improved in data-driven, outcome-based delivery of projects?

In their recent study of productivity in construction, McKinsey Global Institute compares myriad characteristics of the AEC industry against its competitive foil, the manufacturing industry.[25] This is a regular trope that often glosses over the enormous structural differences between the two industry sectors, the most important of which is relative disintegration of the construction supply chain. The largest German automobile manufacturers like Daimler or Volkswagen integrate vast expanses of the networks of fabricators and suppliers upon which they rely, and by virtue of scale and repeat business can control much of the business relationships, including technology. Hochtief, the largest German contractor, has no such leverage, and has to assemble a bespoke project team for every job. When working in the US under their subsidiaries Turner Construction and Clark Builders (two of the largest contractors in the US by themselves) they are part of a network of almost 750,000 companies involved in construction.[26]

Fields of change

McKinsey casts the challenges and opportunities for construction through several lenses, the most provocative of which is what they call digitization, or the use of information technology to improve productivity. And the case for construction is stark, as shown in their mapping of relative adoption of digital technology against productivity growth for a range of industries, shown in

4.4.1 Figure 4.4.1. Advanced manufacturing, not surprisingly, is a strong leader, and construction absolutely dead last.

Thus our friends from the consulting world, citing a $1.6 trillion productivity opportunity in construction, make a series of recommendations about how to improve construction, four of which fall directly within the thesis of this book[27]:

---

25 McKinsey Global Institute (ed.), "Reinventing Construction: A Route to Higher Productivity."
26 See https://www.statisticbrain.com/construction-industry-statistics/.
27 McKinsey Global Institute (ed.), "Reinventing Construction: A Route to Higher Productivity," pp. 8–9.

— **Rewire the contractual framework** away from 'hostile' relationships to those that rely on collaboration via transparency and information exchange.

— **Rethink design and engineering processes** to include continuous cost management and prefabricated systems for standardization.

— **Improve procurement and supply chain management** by increasing transparency, digitizing procurement protocols and leveraging the internet of things to manage supply.

— **Infuse digital technology, new materials and advanced automation** by making BIM universal and providing collaboration infrastructure, as well as new data collection and analysis techniques like drones and laser scanning.

While BIM adoption continues to grow across the world, its contribution to the overall digitization of construction is negligible, as McKinsey suggests. But as computing becomes more ubiquitous (via the cloud), deliverable to the point of work including on the construction site (via mobile technology), and construction information is based upon a central reference and organizing standard (BIM), the transformations of digitization will slowly emerge and their opportunities become apparent. And as the delivery systems and structures of building evolve under the influence of digital technologies, the business models and practices of architecture will need to respond. Architecture should strive to move its tiny dot, a component of the larger AEC industry, up McKinsey's scale — but what does that mean?

Delivery under the influence

Before examining how the structures of architecture practice might evolve in response, let us first posit how the overall delivery structures, within which architects function, may evolve and thereby place demands — or create opportunities — for architects. Those delivery structures are comprised of the contractual frameworks, exchanges of professional responsibility and procedures and protocols within which the owner actuates a building process to obtain an asset. As discussed elsewhere in the text (see Chapter 4.3, "Calibrating Design Results and Outcomes"), most such models, which go by terms like 'Design Bid Build,' 'Construction Manager' or 'Design Build in the Build' in the US and have analogs in other markets, create archetypal roles and responsibilities for each of the key players — owner, designer, builder — and mechanisms for defining information exchange and risk boundaries. These systems have evolved to optimize a particular characteristic of a project: 'Design Bid Build' aims at the lowest construction cost, 'Design Build' creates consolidated responsibility for both design and construction, and 'Construction Manager' intends an early involvement of the builder. Interestingly, no system attempts to optimize outcomes for all of the players in the delivery spectrum. They rather serve to protect the owner from the var-

'Design Bid Build,'
'Construction Manager,'
'Design Build'

4.4.1 McKinsey productivity of construction[1]

United States   **Productivity growth, 2004–14[2]**

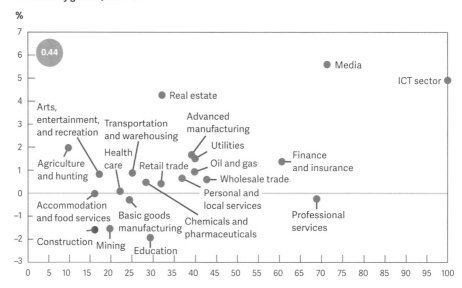

Europe[2, 3]

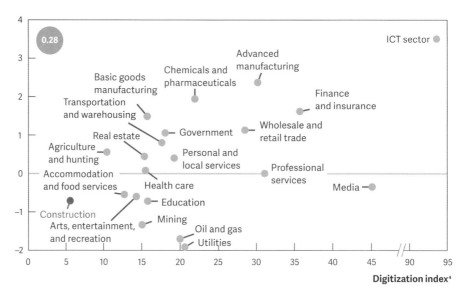

Digitization index[4]

In this chart, the relative lack of digitization in construction is corellated to a lack of productivity.

1   Correlation analysis excludes ICT sector which was a significant outlier in its digitization index value. As a robustness check, we calculated the correlation coefficient for different productivity-growth time periods ranging from 2000–14. Correlation coefficient remains low across time periods.

2   US data are for the private business sector only; Europe data are for the total economy.

3   Europe productivity growth calculated as a simple average of France, Germany, Italy, Spain, Sweden, and the United Kingdom.

4   Based on a set of metrics to assess digitization of assets (8 metrics), usage (11 metrics), and labor (8 metrics); 2015 or latest available data.

Note: Not to scale.

Source: BLS Mulitfactor Productivity database (2018 release); EU KLEMS (2016 release): Digital America: A tale of the haves and have-mores, McKinsey Global Institute, December 2015; Digital Europe: Pushing the frontier, capturing the benefits, McKinsey Global Institute. June 2016. McKinsey Global Institute analsysis

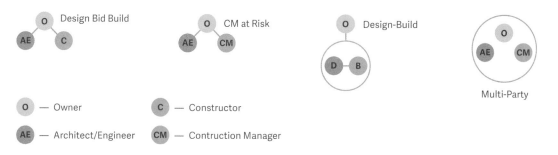

O — Owner

AE — Architect/Engineer

C — Constructor

CM — Contruction Manager

ious perils of the construction process and shift the risk onto the other members of the delivery team. This is no bad strategy in itself — after all, the owner hires these folks to deliver and protect from risk — but it has created, in the modern age, a lot of pathology that degrades progress and productivity.

4.4.2

  What happens when digital technologies like BIM, collaboration infrastructure, big data and analytics, and machine learning finally make it into the industry toolkit? Delivery, in principle, is a function of creating and exchanging information that is then enacted physically by design data moving to the construction site. Those information exchanges are intermediated by the various players, depending on their role, ability to assume risk and agency to act upon it. In a project context where that information is digital, we can assume a new set of characteristics that will change the use of the information and the agency to create it. Imagine a hypothetical job where high-resolution, BIM-organized project data is integrated into the overall design and construction process and the players needed to design and build the job can regularly access, augment, explore and leverage that data for their work. The resulting data infrastructure would have the following characteristics:

A BIM-enabled integrated project

— **Accessibility** Information is indexed, searchable and easily reached by any member of the team for whatever purpose.
— **Transparency** The work of each project contributor would be apparent to all other contributors so that the status of development and level of resolution could influence work in progress.
— **Immediacy** Information can be delivered easily to the most useful point of work in the studio, office, construction trailer, fabrication factory floor or job site.
— **Accuracy** Indexed and organized by principles of BIM (or whatever successor epistemology), project information is connected, related and coordinated and thereby reliable, no longer reliant on human intervention to be properly coordinated.

— **Predictability** Augmented by simulation and analysis, information can be easily tested, verified and used to project future conditions and circumstances.

The resulting free exchange of information[28] and insight lowers the traditional boundaries of control, agency and risk distribution in project delivery, and shifts the agency of the architect who is then free to adjust the business platforms of practice.

Reforming project delivery

The biorhythms of the building industry are slower than those of other types of business. Projects usually take years to complete, and industry change happens over multiple projects. The first stirrings of revolution in project delivery catalyzed by technology began at the outset of BIM in 2004[29] and fourteen years later at this writing the characteristics of a new paradigm — integrated project delivery (IPD) — are just coming into focus. While IPD is an evolving idea that will likely continue to transform as it is refined and the technologies like BIM that support it evolve, several salient components can be seen as indicators of changes to come. As defined by Howard Ashcraft, an attorney and leading proponent of IPD,[30] these are:

— **Restructured business models** based on collaborative decision-making and risk sharing as well as jointly developed goals and measures.
— **Profit at risk dependent on project outcomes** where all profits are paid based on achieving the predetermined characteristics of a successful project.
— **Variable costs without caps** where costs of work are one of many variable measures of success.
— **Few, or no, change orders** unless they are generated by the client.
— **Early involvement of all participants** who agree on the definition of success for the given project.
— **Shared risk and reward** that is a function of project outcomes.
— **Reduced liability** where project players agree not to sue each other.

These characteristics were aptly summed up by John Tocci, a contractor advocate of new project delivery models, on a sign he posts on all his job sites that says: "We all work for the project." This encapsulates the mission of new

28 It is likely that such an environment would also rely on new models of intellectual property that entail licensing and use control rather than strict ownership.
29 CURT, "Collaboration, Integrated Information, and the Project Lifecycle in Building Design, Construction and Operation."
30 Howard Ashcraft, "Integrated Project Delivery: A Prescription for an Ailing Industry," *Construction Law International* 9, no. 4 (2014).

project delivery concepts: aligning the interests of all project participants with those of the project itself dramatically increases the agency, degrees of freedom and capabilities of the entire enterprise, and with it makes success much more likely. Architects probably have the most to gain from these degrees of freedom.

A new role in new delivery models

A consistent characteristic of typical delivery models is sub-optimization: the tendency for each player in the system to prioritize its needs and constraints first, then after those needs are met, turn to those of the project itself. Consider the standard protocols for procuring projects, a template used repeatedly by building industry clients. First, the client might choose an architect, picking from a rich selection of talented designers, based on who charges the lowest total fee. Then the architect prepares the design, and when it is time to choose the builder, the first criterion is the builder's bid — again, lowest first cost. As the builder assembles its team, each subcontractor, supplier and/or fabricator is subject to the same pressure — thus creating a delivery network that is optimized for the owner's first cost, and driving behaviors accordingly.

In new delivery systems underpinned by technology, the architect has a profoundly new agency, if that system extrapolates on Ashcraft's first principles. Once technology empowers an entire team to create and then achieve a set of predetermined, measurable and rewarded goals, questions of division of labor and allocation of risk fade from view. When risks and rewards are collaboratively assumed (and validated through collaborative decision-making supported by much more precise information) the designer's agency is a function of making things happen, and not limited by roles or standards, like the standard of care.

Four directions to extend design reach

Thus architects are free to extend their design reach in numerous directions across the structures of delivery. There are four directions for the expansion of the architect's role and agency and with those expansions, changes in the business models of practice.

4.4.3 **1. Expanded design services** An immediate operating benefit of digitization for architects is the inherent efficiency of technology for design visualization, production optimization and automation of tiresome chores like the generation of specifications and schedules. This is easy and certainly adds to the bottom line — or creates additional resources of time for extra design.[31]

Chapter 4.3 outlined several value expansion opportunities for the architect to extend her agency into services that create value by their correla-

---

31 For a more detailed examination of this theory, see Phillip G. Bernstein, "Intention to Artifact in the Age of High-Resolution Design Representation," in Scott Marble (ed.), *Digital Workflows in Architecture: Designing Design — Designing Assembly — Designing Industry* (Basel: Birkhäuser, 2012).

Extra-mural services

Financial analyst ④		AI developer ④	Analyst ④		Fabricator ④	Furniture designer ④	Data wrangler ④
Feasibility	**Concept**	**Detailed Design**	**Production Design**	**Procure**	**Construction**	**Close-out**	**Occupancy**
(Project origination)	(Program development)	❶ Expanded design scenics			(Construction support)		(Facilities management)
	⓪ Typical services						
(Developer)	❷ Architect as owner						(Owner)
				❸ Architect as builder			

⓪ Traditional "waterfall" phasing
❶ Expanded design services
❷ Architect as owner
❸ Architect as builder
❹ Extra-mural services

tion to outcomes. The limits of such options are only those imposed by her skills and abilities and willingness to shoulder the resulting risk (and convert the resulting reward). When delivery is driven by outcomes and not the commoditized exchange of data, the architect can 'pitch in' wherever her talents can move a project forward, and relationally contracted projects like IPD create a clear field to deliver services.

Even in circumstances where a new delivery model is not contemplated, design is a strategy for establishing the feasibility of a project or optimizing a construction sub-system, each of which can depend on the use of digital tools and predictive algorithms. The resulting business arrangements can be a function of the value of the service provided and not the hours expended in performing that service.

2. The architect as owner Current practices like Alloy Development or Barrett Development (both architect-led developers in New York City) demonstrate that some architects already are willing to step across the owner-architect divide and assume the lead position on projects. This instinct will be

<u>Architects who act as developers</u>

further emboldened by technology. Higher precision in cost estimating and construction scheduling, based on information generated by the architect, will increase the confidence of lenders in project design and give architects the chance to become owners. Predictive analytics, combined with greater insight on comparables and financial performance (data already collected and heavily leveraged by practices like Alloy), will be combined with architect-led development proposals. Technology extends agency, and some firms will choose to control their own destiny by becoming developers themselves.

3. The architect as builder The increased reliance on digital information to drive aspects of building draws the architect closer to construction as it is further industrialized. Outcome-based delivery structures and contracts will divorce the architect from anxieties about her responsibilities for 'means and methods.' A willingness to work closely with builders and fabricators, combined with the critical accelerator of shared risk/reward incentives, creates a virtuous loop of information and insight between architects and builders yielding efficiencies and reliable results, all of which are convertible value propositions. In the next decade we will see architects contributing large design data sets to constructors, joint venturing with specialty sub-system manufacturers, even becoming subcontractors on specialty systems for which they have developed expertise themselves. With the intent<->execution barrier destroyed, architects can willingly venture into the opportunities of making and with it, the resulting rewards.

4. Extra-mural services and businesses Historians like Mario Carpo, Molly Wright Steeson and even Greg Lynn have argued that architects have been responsible for some of the most important computational advances of the modern age,[32] but I would add that ithe profession has largely failed to turn those ideas into businesses. The growing ubiquity of computation in construction gives architects another chance to take the process innovations into new sorts of services or even products that are vessels of architectural agency. Davenport and Kirby[33] argue that a hedge against machine learning replacing knowledge work is to be the first to create the AI platforms themselves, suggesting that if algorithms are playing an important part in your discipline it's in your best interest to be the first to create them. If professionals take responsibility for designing the systems that will eventually replace some or all of their work, they have a better chance of controlling the resulting changes in their roles and responsibilities. There is a tradition of architectural interest here reaching all the way back to 1970 and architect Nicolas Negroponte's MIT Media Lab.[34] McAfee and Brynjolfsson, citing the examples of new firms like Uber, extol the virtues of integrating machine learning,

32 For a good timeline of such developments, see Andrew Goodhouse (ed.), *When is the Digital in Architecture?* (Montreal and Berlin: Canadian Centre for Architecture and Sternberg Press, 2017).
33 Davenport and Kirby, *Only Humans Need Apply: Winners and Losers in the Age of Smart Machines.*
34 Nicholas Negroponte, *The Architecture Machine* (Cambridge, MA: The MIT Press, 1970).

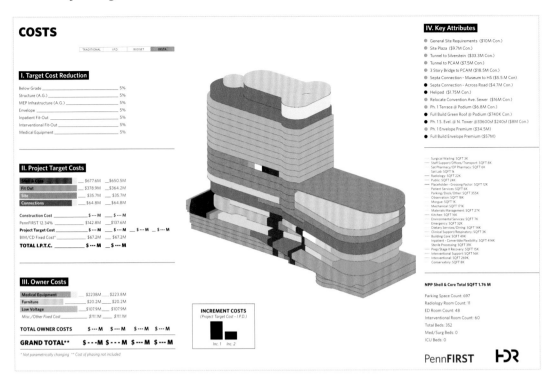

intermediation platforms and heterogeneous collections of users and providers, a proxy for the messy process of orchestrating a building project.[35]
The most advanced work in scripting and algorithmic design continues to
originate in schools of architecture. Given the entrepreneurial, start-up zeit-
geist of the second decade of the twenty-first century, a wave of next-generation solution providers will emerge, led by architects in the vanguard of industry digitization and innovation. Look for architects leading firms that
deliver integrated projects, create next generation tools, or leverage the value of design data in new, useful and profitable ways.

4.4.4

**New levers,
influence, value**

In 2002 I led a business unit at Autodesk, the AEC technology provider, that
decided that the era of computer-aided design (CAD) as the exclusive technology platform for the world's architects and engineers needed to end, and
with that ending came a new idea, building information modeling. Over the
next fifteen years we developed, in parallel, the new technology that was to
become the world standard for BIM and an argument for why it was relevant:
not because the industry needed another shinier toy, but rather that the

35 Andrew McAfee and Erik Brynjolfsson, *Machine, Platform, Crowd: Harnessing Our Digital Future.*

business context of construction needed a new informational basis to dictate the relationships and responsibilities of the players. We worked hard on making the tools appropriate, to define ideas like IPD and industrialized construction because we were convinced that technology's real value lay not in mere efficiencies but in opportunities to break the old rules of roles, responsibilities and risks. Almost twenty years after those first instincts brought about BIM, it is clear that technology can provide architects with both value opportunities and the agency to engage them. The newest tools put both extraordinary capabilities and the potential for integration, which our friends in manufacturing have enjoyed for a long time, at our fingertips. Perhaps someday an integrated design/construction/delivery organization will enjoy the same brand presence, influence and value as their automotive or smartphone counterparts. But at minimum architects have an opportunity, not likely to come again, to reposition themselves in the value chain of the building industry and have the influence over the built environment we believe we deserve.

5

con
clu
sion

Conclusion

In late 2017 as I was finishing the first draft of this book, *The New York Times* published an investigation of skyrocketing construction costs on the subway being built under Grand Central Station. The article described how labor costs on the job were multiples higher than comparable projects elsewhere (even in strong union labor markets like France) and that the cost of union contracts were uncoupled from any performance requirements of the project:

> An accountant discovered the discrepancy while reviewing the budget for new train platforms under Grand Central Terminal in Manhattan. The budget showed that 900 workers were being paid to dig caverns for the platforms as part of a 3.5-mile tunnel connecting the historic station to the Long Island Rail Road. But the accountant could only identify about 700 jobs that needed to be done, according to three project supervisors. Officials could not find any reason for the other 200 people to be there. "Nobody knew what those people were doing, if they were doing anything," said Michael Horodniceanu, who was then the head of construction at the Metropolitan Transportation Authority, which runs transit in New York. The workers were laid off, Mr. Horodniceanu said, but no one figured out how long they had been employed. "All we knew is they were each being paid about $1,000 every day.[1]

Apparently this project was spending $50 million a year of taxpayer money on people just standing around during the construction of that tunnel. Why? How did the MTA's head of construction not notice that he was spending $200,000 each day on nothing? Millions more dollars had been spent on engineering consultants, cost estimators, construction managers and planners, tunneling subcontractors, machine operators, owner-side project managers and contracting officers — all of whom have an excellent idea of how

---

1   Brian M. Rosenthal, "The Most Expensive Mile of Subway Track on Earth," *The New York Times* (2017).

many people it takes to dig a tunnel beneath a dense urban neighborhood — and somehow nobody seemed to notice. Later in the article, an advisor to New York governor Andrew Cuomo explained that labor contracts costs — usually about 50% of a construction project budget — were not negotiated by the client, the MTA, and therefore "(n)obody at the negotiating table is footing the bill."[2]

These sorts of stories amplify the AEC industry's well-deserved (and -documented)[3] reputation for low productivity and, frankly, worse, as anyone who has watched a few episodes of *The Sopranos* can attest. One can be sure that if uncontested costs of any kind — labor or otherwise — were somehow attached to the price of producing every BMW or Chevrolet built the manufacturer would know and prevent the cost of every car from escalating accordingly.

And what, exactly, might this have to do with the thesis of this book, that declares that new technologies change the methods and agency of architecture? One might glibly suggest that what that ill-fated aspect of the tunneling project lacked was someone like an architect taking responsibility for integrating the various parts and pieces into a singular whole, since seeing a project holistically is one of our special talents. Whether a subway station or a building, the need for an integrated view that stitches together the objectives of the project is unquestioned, and spending billions of dollars does not assure that such a transparent view of a project in all its complex glory is going to happen. It is precisely that opportunity — to reassert the agency of design to lead building — that is at the core of the changes discussed here.

Technologies emerge, and surprise us until they are absorbed into the fabric of day-to-day work life. Several decades ago, with the emergence of the World Wide Web, I spent time setting up a crude project collaboration website, complete with file sharing, web-based announcements and email, to serve as the communication infrastructure of a large project in Miami. Today such capabilities would be taken for granted, they are basic 'table stakes' for any building project using even the crudest digital infrastructure. What was important about that effort (which, for the record, was largely unsuccessful) was that it was an attempt by the architects to orchestrate the process and artifacts to increase the likelihood of the design's success.

The newer technologies appearing in the second digital turn are less transactional and more profound, in that we are now reaching a time where the tools are rapidly approaching the real possibility of managing the complexities of making buildings — the numerous interactions, dependencies and decisions in addition to the sheer size and detail needed to represent

2   Ibid.
3   American Institute of Architects, "Reinventing Construction: A Route to Higher Productivity."

even the smallest building. Conceivably, if our friends from the MTA had had access to even rudimentary modeling, accounting analysis and historical data sets about their tunnel, those 200 extra laborers might have never appeared in the first place. Just as it has improved the productivity and quality of other endeavors, the marketplace will press the AEC industry as a whole to leverage computation to improve and meet the challenges of twenty-first century construction. It is inevitable that building design and construction will modernize and follow in the footsteps of the industries that have climbed higher on McKinsey's digitization/productivity curve.

Architects have met the recent several waves of change in the building industry — industrialization, the explosion of specialists, the liability crisis, sustainability, even early CAD — with ambivalence, simultaneously declaring the importance of our design skills while at the same retreating from our earlier positions of integrative leadership as the primary agent of the owner. Design operates at the headwaters of the entire building enterprise, and design information — no matter who might create it — is still the necessary lifeblood of construction. Understanding, controlling and coordinating how this information assures that a design converts into a built artifact will be our central challenge in a world where digital modeling, machine expertise, high resolution data sets and algorithms become part of a modernized building industry. The tools are certainly available and at our beck and call, we only have to decide to use them.

appen dix

Bibliography

Alberti, Leon Battista. *On the Art of Building in Ten Books*. Transl. Joseph Rykwert,
　　Neil Leach and Robert Tavernor. Cambridge, MA: MIT Press, 1988.

Alexander, Christopher. *Notes on the Synthesis of Form*. Cambridge, MA: Harvard
　　University Press, 1964.

Allen, Stan. "The Paperless Studios in Context." In Andrew Goodhouse (CCA) (ed.).
　　When Is the Digital in Architecture? Montreal and Berlin: Sternberg Press,
　　2013. 383–404.

American Institute of Architects. "A201 2007 General Conditions of the Contract for
　　Construction." Washington, DC: American Institute of Architects, 2007. 37.

———. "B101-2017 Standard Form of Agreement between Owner and Architect."
　　Washington, DC: American Institute of Architects, 2017. 23.

———. "The Architect's Voice: Advocating for Our Profession." In *AIA*, edited by
　　AIA. Washington, DC: American Institute of Architects, 2016.

Ansari, Iman. "Eisenman's Evolution: Architecture, Syntax, and New Subjectivity."
　　Arch Daily (2013).

Architects' Council of Europe. *The Architectural Profession in Europe 2016. A Sector
　　Study*. Architects' Council of Europe, 2017. 102.

Ashcraft, Howard. "Integrated Project Delivery: A Prescription for an Ailing
　　Industry." *Construction Law International* 9, no. 4 (2014): 8.

Atkins, James B., and Grant A. Simpson. *Managing Project Risk: Best Practices for
　　Architects and Related Professionals*. Hoboken, NJ: Wiley, 2008.

Baker, Kermit. "How Many Architects Does Our Economy Need?" *ARCHITECT* (05
　　January 2018).

———, Jennifer Riskus et al. *AIA Firm Survey Report: Business of Architecture 2016*.
　　Washington, DC: American Institute of Architects, 2016. 91.

———, ——— (ed.). *Compensation Report 2017*. Washington, DC: American
　　Institute of Architects, 2017. 147.

Bascomb, Neal. *Higher: A Historic Race to the Sky and the Making of a City*. New
　　York, NY: Doubleday, 2003.

Bernstein, Harvey M. "Managing Uncertainty and Expectations in Building Design
　　and Construction." In Harvey M. Bernstein (ed.). *McGraw Hill Smart Market
　　Reports*. New York, NY: McGraw Hill Construction Analytics, 2014. 64.

Bernstein, Phillip G. "Digital Workflows Book Launch." In *100*, edited by Columbia GSAPP Lecture. New York, NY: Columbia University GSAPP, 2013.

———. "Intention to Artifact." In Scott Marble (ed.). *Digital Workflows in Architecture: Designing Design – Designing Assembly – Designing Industry*. Basel: Birkhäuser, 2012.

———. "Money, Value, Architects, Building." *Perspecta* 47, no. MONEY (September 2014): 14–20.

———. "Thinking Versus Making: Remediating Design Practice in the Age of Digital Representation." In Branko Kolarevic and Kevin R. Klinger (ed.). *Manufacturing Material Effects: Rethinking Design and Making in Architecture*. New York, NY: Routledge, 2008.

Bernstein, Phillip, et al. *Goat Rodeo: Practicing Built Environments*. CreateSpace Independent Publishing Platform, 2015.

Biemiller, Lawrence. "At 14, Iconic Building at U. of Cincinnati Is Already a Candidate for Preservation." *The Chronicle of Higher Education* (2010).

Block, Philippe. "Parametricism's Structural Congeniality." *Architectural Design* 86, no. 02 – Parametricism 2.0: Rethinking Architecture's Agenda for the 21st Century. Patrik Schumacher, Editor (2016): 6.

Bradshaw, Dan. "The Rewards and Risks of BIM." *Benchmark Review* 6 (2006). http://www.benchmark-insurance.com/BIM.pdf.

Brynjolfsson, Erik, and Andrew McAfee (ed.). *The Second Machine Age: Work, Progress, and Prosperity in a Time of Brilliant Technologies*. New York, NY: W. W. Norton & Company, 2014.

Buntrock, Dana. *Japanese Architecture as a Collaborative Process: Opportunities in a Flexible Construction Culture*. London, New York, NY: Spon Press, 2001.

Burry, Mark. "Essential Precursors to the Parametricism Manifesto: Antoni Gaudi and Frei Otto." *Architectural Design* 86, no. 02 – Parametricism 2.0: Rethinking Architecture's Agenda for the 21st Century. Patrik Schumacher, Editor (2016): 8.

Carpo, Mario. *The Alphabet and the Algorithm*. Writing Architecture. Cambridge, MA: The MIT Press, 2011.

———. "The Alternative Science of Computation." *e-flux architecture* Artificial Labor, no. 23 (June 2017).

———. *The Second Digital Turn: Design Beyond Intelligence*. Writing Architecture. Cambridge, MA: The MIT Press, 2017.

Computer Integrated Construction Research Program at the Pennsylvania State University. *Building Information Modeling Execution Planning Guide*. State College, PA: The Pennsylvania State University, 2010. 126.

CURT, Construction Users Roundtable. "Collaboration, Integrated Information, and the Project Lifecycle in Building Design, Construction and Operation." In *CURT Whitepapers*, 20: Construction Users Roundtable, 2004.

Davenport, Thomas H., and Julia Kirby (ed.). *Only Humans Need Apply: Winners and Losers in the Age of Smart Machines*. New York, NY: Harper Business, 2016.

Dodge Data and Analytics (ed.). "Optimizing the Owner Organization: The Impact of Policies and Practices on Performance." In *http://analyticsstore.construction.com/OptimizingOwnerOrg.html*. New York, NY: Dodge, 2016.

Domingos, Pedro. *The Master Algorithm: How the Quest for the Ultimate Learning Machine Will Remake Our World*. New York, NY: Basic Books, 2015.

Fischer, M., and M. Schutz. "Construction Planning and Feedback Loops – Analysis of Current Practice." In *Stanford Center for Facilities Engineering Technical Advisory Committee*. Palo Alto, CA: Stanford University, 2017.

Fischer, Martin, Atul Khanzode, Dean P. Reed and Howard W. Ashcraft. *Integrating Project Delivery*. Hoboken, NJ: John Wiley & Sons Inc., 2017. http://onlinelibrary.wiley.com/book/10.1002/9781119179009.

Frey, Carl Benedikt, and Michael A. Osborne. "The Future of Employment: How Susceptible Are Jobs to Computerization." https://www.oxfordmartin.ox.ac.uk/downloads/academic/The_Future_of_Employment.pdf. 1 (2013): 72.

Gerbino, Anthony, Stephen Johnston. *Compass and Rule: Architecture as Mathematical Practice in England, 1500–1750*. Exh. cat. Oxford and New Haven, CT: Museum of the History of Science, Yale University Press and Yale Center for British Art, 2009.

Goldberger, Paul. "Google's New Built-from-Scratch Googleplex." *Vanity Fair* (22 February 2013). https://www.vanityfair.com/news/tech/2013/02/exclusive-preview-googleplex.

Higgin, Gurth, William Neil Jessop and Tavistock Institute of Human Relations London. *Communications in the Building Industry; the Report of a Pilot Study*. 2d ed. London: Tavistock Publications, 1965.

Hill, Kristen, Katherine Copeland and Christian Pikel. *Target Value Delivery: Practitioner Guidebook to Implementation Current State 2016*. Arlington, VA: LEAN Construction Institute, 2016.

Ingalls, Julia. "Architecture Majors Work the Hardest in College, Study Reveals." *Archinet News* (7 February 2017). https://archinect.com/news/article/149990764/architecture-majors-work-the-hardest-in-college-study-reveals.

Internet Legal Research Group. "Salaries of Legal Professionals 2016 (USA)." *Internet Legal Research Group* (2016). https://www.ilrg.com/employment/salaries/.

Ipsen, Erik. "So Many Projects, So Few Architects. How Design Firms Are Filling a Talent Gap." *Crain's New York Business* (15 June 2015).

Jung, Wooyoung, and Ghang Lee. "The Status of BIM Adoption on Six Continents." *International Scholarly and Scientific Research & Innovation* 9, no. 5 (2015): 406–10.

King, Leslie P., and Karen Holmes. "Evolving Practice and the Standard of Care: Sustainability, Security and Everything in Between." *Proceedings of the 54th Annual Meeting of Invited Attorneys – Victor O Schinnerer* (2015): 8.

King, Ross. *Brunelleschi's Dome: How a Renaissance Genius Reinvented Architecture*. New York, NY: Walker & Co., 2000.

Knight, Will. "Biased Algorithms Are Everywhere, and No One Seems to Care." *MIT Technology Review* (12 July 2017). https://www.technologyreview.com/s/608248/biased-algorithms-are-everywhere-and-no-one-seems-to-care/.

Krolak, Keith. "Order of Public Building Phases." In *MLIT*, Design phases, with English translation by K. Krolak. Tokyo: MLIT, 2018.

Leicher, Matt. "Lawyers Per Capita by State." In *The Last Gen X American*, 2016.

Lewis-Kraus, Gideon. "The Great A.I. Awakening." *The New York Times Magazine* (14 December 2016).

Marble, Scott. *Digital Workflows in Architecture: Designing Design – Designing Assembly – Designing Industry*. Basel: Birkhäuser, 2012.

McAfee, Andrew, and Erik Brynjolfsson (ed.). *Machine, Platform, Crowd: Harnessing Our Digital Future*. New York, NY: W. W. Norton & Company, 2017.

McKinsey Global Institute (ed.). "Reinventing Construction: A Route to Higher Productivity." In *https://www.mckinsey.com/industries/capital-projects-and-infrastructure/our-insights/reinventing-construction-through-a-productivity-revolution*. McKinsey & Company, 2017.

———. *Solving the Productivity Puzzle: The Role of Demand and the Promise of Digitization.* McKinsey, 2018. 160.

Moneo, Rafael. *The Solitude of Buildings: Kenzo Tange Lecture*. Cambridge, MA: Harvard Graduate School of Design, 1985.

Munhall, Dale L. "Standard of Care: Confronting the Errors-and-Omissions Taboo up Front." *AIA Best Practices* (February 2011): 3.

National Council of Architectural Registration Boards (NCARB) (ed.). "2012 NCARB National Practice Analysis of Architecture." Washington, DC: NCARB, 2012. 325.

———. "Legislative Guidelines and Model Law – Model Regulations 2016–2017." Washington, DC: NCARB, 2016.

———. "NCARB by the Numbers." Washington, DC: NCARB, 2016.

Negroponte, Nicholas. *The Architecture Machine*. Cambridge, MA: The MIT Press, 1970.

Novelli, Nicholas, Justin Shultz and Anna Dyson. *Development of a Modeling Strategy for Adaptive Multifunctional Solar Energy Building Envelope Systems*. Alexandria, VA: Society for Computer Simulation International, 2015. 35–42.

Osterwalder, Alexander, Yves Pigneur and Tim Clark. *Business Model Generation: A Handbook for Visionaries, Game Changers, and Challengers*. Hoboken, NJ: Wiley, 2010.

Petroski, Henry. *To Forgive Design: Understanding Failure*. Cambridge, MA: Belknap Press of Harvard University Press, 2012.

Rampell, Catherine. "Want a Job? Go to College, and Don't Major in Architecture." *The New York Times* (5 January 2012).

Rittel, Horst W. J., and Melvin M. Webber. "Dilemmas in a General Theory of Planning." *Policy Sciences* 4, no. 2 (1973): 155–69.

Rosenthal, Brian M. "The Most Expensive Mile of Subway Track on Earth." *The New York Times* (2017).

Rowe, Peter G. "A Priori Knowledge and Heuristic Reasoning in Architectural Design." *Journal of Architectural Education* 36, no. 1 (1982): 18–23.

Royal Institute of British Architects. "RIBA Plan of Work." https://www.ribaplanof-work.com/PlanOfWork.aspx. London: RIBA, 2013.

Scharphie, Mia. *Emerging Modes of Architectural Practice*. Northeastern University School of Architecture, 2015.

Schumacher, Patrik. "Parametricism Manifesto." 2008.

Schumacher, Patrik, and ebrary Inc. *Parametricism 2.0: Rethinking Architecture's Agenda for the 21st Century*. 2016. http://site.ebrary.com/lib/yale/Doc?id=11251744.

Singapore Building Construction Authority. "About Corenet" (2013). https://www.bca.gov.sg/newsroom/others/pr31102013_BCAA.pdf.

Susskind, Richard E., and Daniel Susskind. *The Future of the Professions: How Technology Will Transform the Work of Human Experts*. Oxford: Oxford University Press, 2015.

Tombesi, Paolo. "On the Cultural Separation of Design Labor." In Peggy Deamer and Phillip G. Bernstein (ed.). *Building (in) the Future: Recasting Labor in Architecture*. New York, NY: Princeton Architectural Press, 2010. 117–36.

Vitruvius Pollio. *Vitruvius: The Ten Books on Architecture*. Transl. M. H. Morgan. New York, NY: Dover Publications, 1960.

Yankelovich, David. "Corporate Priorities: A Continuing Study of the New Demands on Business." In *Daniel Yankelovich Inc*. Stamford, CT: Daniel Yakelovich Inc., 1972.

Illustration Credits

The original drawings for this book were conceived by the author and designed by the graphic designer Miriam Bussmann. Images and figures not otherwise created by the author were provided courtesy of the following sources:

Alloy Development   3.4.8

American Institute of Architects   4.1.3[1]

Anchin, Block & Anchin, LLP (Brian Kenet)   4.1.2

Apicella Bunton Architects   3.3.2[2]

Archive.org   2.2.1[3], 3.5.1[4]

Autodesk Inc.   2.2.3, 2.2.4, 2.2.5, 2.3.1, 2.5.3, 2.5.4, 3.1.3, 3.2.2

Buro Happold Engineers   3.4.6

Chait & Company Architects   3.2.1[5]

Eisenman Architects   3.4.2, 3.4.3

Gluck+   3.4.4

Greg Lynn FORM   3.1.2

HDR   4.4.4

Iwan Baan Studio   2.5.2[6]

Krolak, Keith   3.3.2[7]

McKinsey Global Institute   4.4.1[8]

Newman Architects   2.3.4

Pelli Clarke Pelli Architects   0.1, 3.4.5, 4.2.4

---

1   Baker, Kermit, Jennifer Riskus et al. *AIA Firm Survey Report: Business of Architecture 2016*. Washington, DC: American Institute of Architects, 2016.
2   Derived from a project schedule provided by the architects.
3   From *L'architettura di Leon Batista Alberti, 1565*, found at https://archive.org/details/larchitettura00albe.
4   From *Di Lucio Vitruuio Pollione De architectura libri dece, 1521*, found at https://archive.org/stream/gri_33125008262210#page/n133/mode/2up.
5   Derived from "Employee Handbooks Starting from Scratch" as provided by Chait & Company Architects.
6   © Iwan Baan Studio.
7   K. Krolak provided information, including translations, regarding the phasing of Japanese architectural processes.
8   McKinsey Global Institute. *Solving the Productivity Puzzle: The Role of Demand and the Promise of Digitization*. McKinsey, 2018. P. 72.

9   Computer Integrated Construction Research Program at the Pennsylvania State University. *Building Information Modeling Execution Planning Guide*. State College, PA: The Pennsylvania State University, 2010. P. i.

10 Novelli, Nicholas, Justin Shultz, Anna Dyson. *Development of a Modeling Strategy for Adaptive Multifunctional Solar Energy Building Envelope Systems*. Alexandria, VA: Society for Computer Simulation International, 2015.

11 As published in Gerbino, Anthony, Stephen Johnston. *Compass and Rule: Architecture as Mathematical Practice in England, 1500–1750*. Exh. cat. Oxford and New Haven, CT: Museum of the History of Science, Yale University Press, and Yale Center for British Art, 2009.

12 Mia Scharphie, *Emerging Modes of Architectural Practice*. Northeastern University School of Architecture, 2015.

13 Based on a diagram provided by the firm in 2007.

14 Paolo Tombesi, "On the Cultural Separation of Design Labor," in *Building (in) the Future: Recasting Labor in Architecture*, ed. Peggy Deamer and Phillip G. Bernstein. New York: Princeton Architectural Press, 2010.

15 http://www.vitroglazings.com/en-US/Resources/Tools-Design-Resources/Calculation-Tools.aspx.

16 Brunelleschi, Modello architettonico della lanterna della cupola, 1430–46. Museo dell'Opera del Duomo, Florence. https://upload.wikimedia.org/wikipedia/commons/4/49/Filippo_brunelleschi_%28attr.%29%2C_modello_architetton-ico_della_lanterna_della_cupola%2C_1430-46.JPG.

17 X-48B during test flight at Edwards AFB. https://commons.wikimedia.org/wiki/File:X-48B_during_test_flight_at_Ed-wards_AFB.jpg

About the Author

Phillip G. Bernstein FAIA RIBA LEED AP ©

Phillip G. Bernstein is Associate Dean and Senior Lecturer at the Yale University School of Architecture, where he has been a member of the faculty since 1989. He received his Bachelor of Arts (honors) from Yale College, where he studied architecture with additional concentrations in computer science and philosophy, and his Master of Architecture also from Yale. He created and teaches Yale's curriculum in Professional Practice.

Prior to his current appointment he was a Vice President at the technology company Autodesk, where he helped lead the company's technology strategy for the building industry, with particular focus on the shift from computer-aided drafting to building information modeling (BIM). Prior to Autodesk Phil was a principal at Pelli Clarke Pelli Architects, where he helped manage some of the firm's most complex projects including the North Terminal at Washington National Airport, the Practice Integration Building at the Mayo Clinic, and the Lerner Research Center at the Cleveland Clinic. He consults, writes and lectures extensively about practice and technology issues, and has been published in *Architectural Record, Architecture, Architecture+Urbanism, Design Intelligence, Fast Company, Fortune* and *Perspecta* and quoted in *The Economist, Vanity Fair, Dwell* and *The Wall Street Journal*. Phil is co-editor of *Building (In) The Future: Recasting Labor in Architecture,* published in 2010 by Princeton Architectural Press, as well as *BIM in Academia: Technology's Implications for Practice and the Academy* in 2011 by Yale School of Architecture.

Phil was the executive responsible for Autodesk's Waltham AEC Headquarters project, which received more than 14 architectural awards including those from the American Institute of Architects, *Business Week/Architectural Record*, the Association of General Contractors and *Interiors* Magazine, and he was honored twice by *DesignIntelligence* as one of the "30 Most Admired Educators in Architecture." He is a Fellow of the American Institute of Architects and is licensed to practice in California.

Key Terms and Names

The author and the publisher would like to thank Autodesk, Inc. for their support of this book.

Graphic design, layout and typesetting Miriam Bussmann, Berlin
Editor for the Publisher Andreas Müller, Berlin
Proofreading Elizabeth Kugler, Wayland, Mass.
Production Bettina Chang, Berlin

Paper Condat matt Perigord, 135 g/m²
Printing optimal media GmbH, Röbel/Müritz

Library of Congress Control Number: 2018955815

Bibliographic information published by the German National Library
The German National Library lists this publication in the Deutsche Nationalbibliografie
detailed bibliographic data are available on the Internet at http://dnb.dnb.de.
This publication is also available as an e-book (ISBN PDF 978-3-0356-1044-4).

© 2018 Birkhäuser Verlag GmbH, Basel
P.O. Box 44, 4009 Basel, Switzerland
Part of Walter de Gruyter GmbH, Berlin/Boston

Printed on acid-free paper produced from chlorine-free pulp. TCF ∞
Printed in Germany

ISBN 978-3-0356-1188-5

9 8 7 6 5 4 3 2 1   www.birkhauser.com